D1155936

RECEIVED

LIBERAL STUDIES,
UPPER DIVISION

STATE

BROCKPORT, N. Y.

WRITING THE MODERN MAGAZINE ARTICLE

WRITING THE MODERN MAGAZINE ARTICLE

BY MAX GUNTHER

THE WRITER, INC. • BOSTON • PUBLISHERS

COPYRIGHT © 1968, 1973, 1976 BY MAX GUNTHER

Third Edition

"Is Television the Answer for Our Crowded Courts?" originally appeared in *TV Guide,* March 25, 1972. Reprinted by permission from TV GUIDE ® Magazine. Copyright © 1972 by Triangle Publications, Inc., Radnor, Pennsylvania.

"Man Versus Insect" originally appeared in *Travel & Leisure,* July 1975. Copyright © 1975 American Express Publishing Corporation. Reprinted by permission.

"Computers: Their Built-In Limitations" originally appeared in *Playboy* Magazine, October 1967. Copyright © 1967 by HMH Publishing Co., Inc. Reprinted by permission.

Library of Congress Cataloging in Publication Data

Gunther, Max, 1927–
    Writing the modern magazine article.

    1. Authorship.   2. Journalism.   I. Title.
    PN147.G8   1973   808'.066'07   73-7750
    ISBN 0-87116-102-8

Printed in the United States of America

CONTENTS

PART FOUR / CASE HISTORIES

INTRODUCTION

Wanted: almost unlimited numbers of men and women. Qualifications: must have a lively interest in people and the world in general, a fondness for the written word, a capacity to work alone, and a typewriter. College degree not necessary; high school diploma helpful but not strictly necessary either. Pleasant working conditions. No commuting. Generous pay.

As far as I know, this ad never appeared in a newspaper help-wanted column. But its essence appears every day in magazine editorial meetings throughout the United States— indeed, throughout the English-speaking world. It is a plea for good nonfiction or article writers. Magazine editors are crying for them.

"There simply aren't enough of you," the editor of a major family magazine told me recently. Hearing this made me feel good, of course. I make my living by writing magazine articles, and it's nice in any trade to hear that you're in demand. All the same, I harbor no fear that by writing this book I'll unduly increase the competition against me and get myself pushed out of the market. The market is so big that such fears aren't reasonable. The market is absolutely enormous, in fact, and is growing faster than it ever grew in any other period of recent history. There could be ten times as many article writers in existence as there actually are, and every one of them (the good ones, that is) would be welcomed in editorial offices. Literally millions of words of nonfiction are printed in magazines each month, and many of those words are simply space-fillers printed out of desperation because the editors couldn't buy what they really wanted.

A new world of magazines

There has been some pessimistic talk about the magazine business in recent years. The deaths of magazines such as *Life, Look* and *The Saturday Evening Post* have led some observers to think the industry is dying. Don't believe it. The industry is actually in excellent health.

Rather than dying, it is going through a metamorphosis. It is something like a forest undergoing some long-term change in climate or soil conditions. Some large old trees have been unable to withstand the change and have died, and the loud crashes made by their falling have led some observers to believe the whole forest is sick. But the observers have not observed carefully enough. Where the old giants fell, robust young trees are springing up in their places.

I will admit I have had to dodge nimbly, on occasion, to get out of the way of all those falling trees. I was writing for *Collier's* when it died many years ago, and then for *Coronet,* and later for the *Post.* Each time a magazine died, I experienced a momentary feeling of panic. I thought, "Well, there goes 20% of my income, there goes 50%." I gave gloomy lectures to my wife and children on the necessity for belt-tightening. But in every case, my frightened predictions of lost income turned out to be wrong. Whenever an old magazine vanished, I found newer—often more exciting—magazines to work for.

As a matter of fact—and this seems like a mad paradox until you examine it closely—the people working in the magazine-article field now seem to have more work in their assignment backlogs than at any time in recent history. Why is this? I think it is a direct result of the pessimistic talk. Some veteran article writers—particularly those who became too closely identified with a single defunct magazine—have fled the field in fear; while many potential writers have been reluctant to enter it. The result is that there are relatively few of us left. In fact, *there are fewer than the editors need.*

Ponder this intriguing fact. I assume you have picked up this book because you are interested in writing magazine articles. I assume also that you consider yourself a beginner in some sense. Perhaps you have never tried to write or sell an article before, or perhaps you have sold a few and now wish to aim at higher-paying markets. As is perfectly natural, you wonder what chances a beginner has to break into these markets. I can tell you with utter honesty that, provided you learn your writing craft well, your chances are very, very good.

What has happened is that the old "general" magazines, so-called, have been dying. The reasons for this are extremely complex (actually, no two observers agree on the reasons), and I won't take time to go into them here. In place of the general magazines, "specialized" magazines have been springing up. These are the markets at which you will aim your shots. We will spend considerable time in this book talking about the problems of aiming: the trick of "feeling" ideas to see which ones fit which magazines, the techniques of slanting and focusing articles, and so on. Your life may be somewhat more complicated than were the lives of article writers, say, twenty years ago. You have perhaps a little more to learn. But your life as a writer won't be any less rewarding, either in terms of money or in terms of creative satisfaction.

Some of the newer magazines are "specialized" only in a broad sense. A stellar example is *Playboy,* founded in the mid-1950s and now one of the most successful magazines in history. It is specialized in that it speaks to a certain type of male readership—but within its self-imposed limits it can cover an enormous range of article subjects. I've written *Playboy* pieces on the stock market, on computers, on genetics: a broad variety of topics. Slightly more specialized is the newer *Penthouse*—but I've written stock-market articles for that magazine too. Still newer are *Oui* (a *Playboy* offshoot) and *Ms.*, each of which can handle a broad subject range as long as the writer pays attention to the special editorial slant.

More narrowly specialized magazines abound. There are regional and city magazines. There are magazines devoted to particular cultural activities, hobbies, political viewpoints, industries, professions. There are magazines about health, money-making opportunities, entertainment media (look at the huge success of *TV Guide*, for instance). The variety, and the article writer's opportunities, are enormous.

Potentially printable

I happened to be sitting in an editor's office recently while he was talking on the phone to his magazine's chief accountant. The editor's article budget for the coming year—the amount of money he'd be allowed to spend in buying articles—had been increased over the previous year's budget. Talking to the accountant about this, the editor sounded grateful and happy. But when he put down the phone his smile evaporated.

"You know," he said, "it's a sad state of affairs. Here I sit with all this money to hand out. Two thousand dollars for a piece, twenty-five hundred, three thousand. Nice big juicy checks, just itching to be mailed. You'd think I'd have great crowds of writers clamoring for the money, you'd think I'd be buried in manuscripts. But it isn't happening. The potentially printable articles that come in here are just a trickle."

Oh, sure, he got enough trash in each day's mail to fill a wheelbarrow. But the *potentially printable* stories—manuscripts from people who had taken the trouble to learn what editors want—these were as scarce as diamonds.

So you see there's an enormous hungry market waiting out there for you. Thousands of magazines big and small. Thousands of editors, sitting in their offices with checkbooks ready. Hoping they'll hear from you. Will they?

Setting your own pace

Well, why not? One of the beauties of magazine article writing is that you can go at it as hard or as light as you like. You make your own schedule, you fit it into whatever life you're living. You can write one article a year or ten or a couple of dozen. You can work at night, or in the early morning, or on your lunch hour or on board a commuter train or in the kitchen when the kids are in school. You can write a short, quick story for a hundred dollars or so, or you can invest more time and aim for the big $1,000-and-up markets. You can think of article writing as strictly a spare-time, extra-cash operation, or if you wish you can harbor in the back of your mind the thought that you may one day want to adopt it as your full-time occupation.

You can make money at it. You can have a lot of fun too. The article writer gets out into the world, out where the action is. He talks to all kinds of people: big people and little, important people and obscure, the sane and the crazy. He is an observer of human life. He is seldom bored. More often he is excited, amused, inspired. He wakes up at night grinning. And sometimes he doesn't go to bed at all but stays up all night because the world has become too interesting to blot out with sleep.

It isn't hard to learn the article writing craft. You need the willingness to work and the patience to stick with it. Behind that, you need what used to be called a "way with words." Most article writers were interested in words when they were kids. In school, they did well in English. They were editors of school newspapers or yearbooks. After school, some got jobs as reporters or advertising copywriters, but others drifted into unrelated fields and grew frustrated and became article writers so they could get close to words again. They aren't Hemingways or Faulkners (though some, in my opinion, are better)—but all are men and women who enjoy manipulating words and, through hard work and practice, have become good at it.

Some write articles full time and earn $25,000 to $50,000 a year. Some write part time and add their article checks to income from regular jobs or other sources. I've never met one of them who wasn't happy.

This book is my invitation to you: won't you join us?

WRITING THE MODERN MAGAZINE ARTICLE

PART ONE

Preparation

1

FINDING ARTICLE IDEAS

Have you ever suggested an article idea to an editor and received a rejection slip in reply? Of course. A short, polite rejection letter? Of course. So have I. So has everybody who ever tried to sell articles to magazines on a free-lance basis. These short, hasty little communications are facts of the article writer's life—and the fiction writer's too, for that matter.

But have you ever received, instead, a long and detailed letter in which the editor explained precisely why .he didn't like your article idea? Not often? Neither have I, neither has anybody. Long rejection letters are rare. They are rare for very good and very interesting reasons.

One reason, of course, is that editors lack time to write many long letters. Another reason is that, odd though it may seem at first glance, *editors don't always know exactly why they're rejecting an idea*.

Signposts and instincts

A good editor approaches an article idea subjectively as well as objectively. Sure, he can reject some writers' proposals for objective reasons alone: the writer is semi-literate, the idea was published in a competing magazine last week, the subject matter is offensive, and so on. But the good ideas, the best ones, the ones he nibbles and chews in his mind the longest, appeal or don't appeal for largely subjective reasons— reasons he can't adequately explain to anybody, even himself. He sizes up an idea largely by its "feel." Through long practice, but without really knowing how he does it, he knows instinctively that an idea "feels" either right or wrong for his particular magazine. The magazine employs him as an editor because he is good at doing this.

The right idea . . .

If this is the case, how can an article writer aim his shots? It isn't as hard as it may sound. With a little basic knowledge and some practice, the writer can develop a talent for feeling ideas, too. In fact, you *must* develop the talent if you want to break into this business and make any kind of headway in it. Without it, all your shots will be in the dark. Some may hit a target. Most won't.

In a normal day, if you talk to a normal number of people and read a normal amount of newsprint, at least ten possible article ideas will suggest themselves to you. That's seventy a week, three hundred a month. These are little fragments of subject matter that interest you: a personal adventure somebody tells you about, a new scientific discovery you read about in the paper. They are germs of article ideas, but only germs. If you tried to write query letters about all three hundred each month, you'd bury yourself in useless work—and, worse yet, you'd anger the editors on whose desks you loaded all this chaff. You have to be selective. Among those three hundred germs of ideas there may be one—just one—that can be developed into a full-bodied article idea. You have to know how to pick it out. You must develop the ability to feel all those possibilities as they drift by, until finally one hits you hard and you say, "This is a story."

What does a good idea feel like? To start with its general characteristics:

1) *It feels big.* It is an idea that has relevance to the lives of many people. It asks a question many people ask, or it deals with some area of common human experience.

I once met a man who had served time in prison and who wanted me to collaborate on an article about one of his experiences. He had been involved in a prison riot in which three men were killed and scores injured. As he told it to me, it was a dramatic and gory tale. But I rejected the idea. It didn't feel big enough. Though the prison was big and the riot was big, it simply didn't seem to me that many readers would find the story relevant to their own lives, their own problems. This story might have sold to one of the lowest-paying men's magazines that specialize in gore for its own sake, but not to a big national magazine.

The day after I talked to the ex-convict, I happened to be sitting around in *True*'s offices when the editors were mulling over another story about another riot. This was a much smaller riot, in a town hardly anybody had ever heard of. Nobody was killed in this little riot, and almost all the injuries were slight. Yet the idea had that solid feeling of bigness. The riot in question was a racial riot in a small Southern town. A writer who lived near the town proposed to tell the story of the riot in detail, and, in the telling, probe the national issues of civil rights and racial unrest in general. Here was a story that would mean something to millions of people. Yes: though the focus of subject matter was small, the idea was big.

2) *It feels necessary.* Almost every big-magazine article carries within it a built-in excuse for its existence—a reason or set of reasons that the writer and editor give the reader to tell him why he should read it, why he should care. Bigness is part of the reason, but not all of it. The reader must be told why he should care right now. Why wasn't he presented with this article last year, five years ago? What's so important about it *today?*

I once had a partly formed idea for an article on anesthesia. The subject was big enough; almost everybody in America has been anesthetized, or knows somebody who has, and almost everybody has some curiosity about anesthetics and how they work and whether they're safe. But the idea didn't feel compellingly necessary. The article could have been written in 1940, or I could wait and write it in 1980. Why *this* year? Who cared?

To put it another way, presenting a reader with an article is something like opening a conversation. Suppose you and I met on a street corner and I said, "Good morning. Did you know that there are more than five hundred different kinds of anesthetics available today?" You'd nod politely and edge away. You'd think I was crazy. I haven't given you a reason for telling you about anesthetics on this particular morning. My words sound *unnecessary*. To start the conversation more sensibly, I ought to say, "Boy, did I have a weird experience at the dentist's this morning! He gave me one of those new anesthetics. . . ." You may be bored stiff as I ramble on, but at least you know why I want you to listen.

Thus I knew it would be a waste of time to query an editor about my anesthesia idea in its early half-baked form. I worried about the idea for a long time. Finally, one day, I read a little newspaper item about a Russian doctor who claimed to have produced instant sleep by shooting a tiny electric current through a patient's brain. Curious, I phoned an anesthetist in a local hospital and asked what he knew about this. He knew quite a lot. In fact, he said, a lot of quiet experimentation was going on in the field of electrical anesthesia, which seemed to offer certain advantages over older methods such as gas and injections.

Instantly I was jolted by the wake-up alarm that every article writer carries in his brain. It shouted, "Story!" Yes, now the idea had that feeling of being necessary. I could tell readers that the century-old anesthesia business was on the verge of startling new discoveries. I had a compelling reason for telling him about the business at that particular time. I sold the idea, and then the article, to a major national magazine.

3) *It feels whole.* It has a quality of compactness and unity; it is a single, solid thing, not a diffuse cloud.

This is largely a matter of focus and is probably the hardest single lesson for a beginning article writer to learn. At first glance, a paradox seems to be involved: how can an idea be big and yet compact at the same time? The paradox is not real, however; and if you understand why not, you understand the feeling of wholeness.

Through most of my article-writing life, for no reason that I can name, I've been interested in the subject of missing persons. Why do people disappear, where do they go, what happens to them? As a potential article idea, this has the required bigness but not the feeling of wholeness. It's too diffuse. It has too many parts, too widely scattered.

How can I solve this problem? By narrowing my point of view, focusing on a small segment of the subject. But doesn't this destroy the feeling of bigness? No, for I can wrap the big subject inside the small one.

I've done this three times so far with the diffuse missing-persons subject. My latest idea was to tell the story of an anguished father whose son disappeared from college, and who closed his business to help the police hunt for the boy. This idea had the wholeness; it dealt with a single episode, mainly with a single man, the father. But it also had the size, for while talking about the father's lonely hunt I could bring in pieces of the larger subject. I could talk about police missing persons bureaus—how efficient they are, how they work—and then answer some of the general questions people might have about missing persons. I could give them general information by showing them a hunt actually in progress.

Yes, this idea had it all. I sold it to *True.*

The right audience

But even if an idea has all three of these key elements—even if it feels big, necessary, whole—you can still waste a lot of time with it if you send it to the wrong magazine. Each magazine has a different group of readers and talks to them in a different way. Each editor, by living his life around the magazine and soaking himself in its attitudes and ambitions, comes to feel the subtle differences between his magazine and all others.

The differences may be extremely subtle, but they do exist. *Playboy, Esquire* and *Penthouse* are all men's magazines and they are quite similar on a first quick reading. But they are dissimilar deep down, and an idea that may feel just right for one would feel totally wrong for the other three. I believe that only *True* would have bought my story about the father and his missing son. And again, *McCall's, Good Housekeeping, Redbook* and other women's magazines seem similar but definitely are not. A few magazines still being published are called "general" magazines, but they aren't really. Each has its own distinct personality.

Thus it does little good to shoot out ideas broadside, sending each to twenty or thirty magazines. It may even do harm. After a while, when an editor has received a long series of unacceptable ideas from you, he'll get grumpy. He'll know you're broadsiding him, wasting his time with ideas that you haven't carefully tailored for his particular magazine. He'll get so he winces at the sight of your letterhead. Several times in my career, I've worked briefly as a fill-in editor for magazines that were shorthanded, and I've often seen this saddening process in action. Once a senior editor sent a messenger to my office with, among other things, an article query from a writer who had been trying to break into that magazine for years. The editor hadn't even read the query. He had clipped onto it a memo to me: "Let me know if you see anything here. You probably won't. This guy never had an idea for us yet." By sending in too many queries that really should have gone elsewhere, the writer had hurt his chances at that magazine and probably at others. It was too bad. He wrote well.

Of course, there are occasional supersize ideas—editors call them "blockbusters"—that would fit into any magazine published. If, for example, you could latch onto a scientist's exclusive story about a bona fide anti-cancer vaccine, you would have an idea so valuable that major magazines would send editors to your home to beg and bid for it. This idea would have more than bigness. It would have enormity. But few ideas are that big. The average idea feels "right" at only a few magazines, or maybe only at one. The best procedure is to send it to the one or two highest-paying magazines where it seems to fit; and then, if they reject it, try some secondary markets—house organs and the like. If that trail peters out, try to rethink the idea for a different set of magazines.

How can you tell what idea feels right for what magazine? There is only one way I know of: read the magazines. Pick the magazines that attract you most, the ones you'd like to see your by-line in, the ones that seem to say the kinds of things you want to say. Then read every issue of those magazines religiously, cover to cover. Don't try to do this with more than a dozen of them; the quality of your understanding is more important than the quantity of reading. After a while, you'll get a feeling for each magazine—the same feeling the editors have. When a good idea comes by, you'll know almost instinctively what magazine, if any, it belongs to. If it doesn't feel quite right for any of them, you'll have a basis for tinkering with it, reslanting it until it does belong somewhere.

It is impossible to overstress the importance of reading your hoped-for markets. Astounding numbers of beginning writers don't. They appear to judge a magazine by its cover, merely guessing at the editorial requirements. The subtleties of a magazine's personality simply can't be gleaned from its cover or from a quick flip-through.

Patience may be one of the article writer's most important virtues. You need to have the patience to understand a magazine thoroughly before you begin submitting ideas to it, and the patience to let ideas ferment and develop in your head until they feel right.

I've had one idea in my head for more than five years. It has to do with college social attitudes. It's slightly wrong for every magazine I can think of. So it sits in my head, an idea without a home.

I'll sell it one day, though. I'll find a way to reshape it. I'll nudge it ever so slightly, and suddenly it'll feel just right for *TV Guide* or *Better Homes* or some magazine not yet invented.

Optimism is another necessary trait for article writers. I believe—I can't prove, I only believe—that every good idea eventually finds a home somewhere.

Making ideas come to you

"Where do you get all your ideas?" This question has been thrown at me often in two decades of free-lance nonfiction writing, but until recently I wasn't very good at answering it. I could only mumble, "Oh, ideas just pop into my head. Who knows where an idea comes from?"

Today I think I have some more specific and satisfactory answers to offer. I sat down one day and asked myself: Where have your best ideas come from? If you want a hot article idea next year or in 1985, where will you start looking?

I went back through my files to 1956, the year I sold my first free-lance effort to the old *Saturday Evening Post,* and tried to reconstruct the births and maturings of my favorite ideas. Whenever memory allowed, I jotted down what I was doing at the time the idea came to me, what the source was, what state of alertness or curiosity made me think, "Aha!

Idea!" I've now put together a short list of rules that I will impose on myself when I next need an idea. Instead of just waiting for ideas to come from nowhere, a nonfiction writer should:

1) *Talk to people*. Go out of your way to find them. Go to parties even though you hate parties. Go to school board meetings. Talk to people who sit next to you on trains and planes, in diners, on park benches. Do anything that will get you into communication with other men and women.

Solitude is useful sometimes during the actual writing process, but as a means of generating ideas, it seems valueless. I honestly can't recall a single good idea that ever came to me while I was simply sitting or ambling around alone, staring into space.

Some of my most profitable ideas have sprung from conversations with other people. A remark by an acoustical engineer led to an article on the science of sound, which I sold to *Playboy*. A rambling talk with a television sales executive sowed the seed of a three-part *TV Guide* report on TV's problems with sex.

2) *Read newspapers hungrily*. Radio and TV news reports aren't nearly detailed enough. Only a newspaper can give you the depth, the background, the odd sidelights that can trigger a salable idea. A nonfiction writer should read at least one good, solid metropolitan paper every day, from front page to back.

A *New York Times* obituary of an industrial inventor led me to the first article I ever sold to *True,* back in 1958. Over the next twelve years I was to sell well over a hundred more pieces to *True*—and, needless to say, I still read obits. Similarly, I plow through the *Times's* food-and-fashion page and its national weather column every day, though neither section contains much that interests me personally. In the fashion section one day, I read an offhand reference that blossomed into a *Ladies' Home Journal* story on runaway wives, and an equally casual remark in the weather column became a *True* piece on scientific attempts to control weather.

3) *Read magazines*—not just those that attract you personally or those you hope to write for, but also the unfamiliar ones, the ones that operate beyond your normal range of interests. By reading an unfamiliar magazine and finding out what its editors and writers are thinking about these days, you can trigger fresh thoughts in your own head.

I don't normally read magazines that deal with investment, but one day on an airplane I borrowed a Wall Street trade journal from the man sitting next to me. Its letters column contained a humorous note about a goofy new way to predict what the stock market will do, and a month later I sold *Playboy* a piece on oddball market-playing techniques. Similarly, I'm not a coin collector, but a magazine devoted to the hobby once gave me an idea for an article about gold, which I sold to *True*.

4) *Never scorn an idea because it is "publicity."* Nearly every big and medium-sized company, college, hospital and government agency has a publicity chief, usually called the news director or public relations director. This man's or woman's job is to get the organization favorably mentioned in the press. It is considered chic in some writers' circles to sneer at publicity people, on the ground that everything they say is self-serving. This attitude seems dumb to me. Publicity may be self-serving, but it can also be interesting.

If you are an idea-hungry nonfiction writer, you should get to know the publicists in companies and institutions near you. They will gladly mail you news of their organizations and work. Listen to them with care. They may provide you with an idea for an article.

A publicity man working for a company that made insect repellent gave me the idea for a *Travel & Leisure* story on mosquitoes. A college publicity woman planted the seed of a *Playboy* piece on the annual national campus manhunt in which businesses try to grab the brightest graduates. These publicists dealt with me because they hoped to get the product or college mentioned in print (which, in fact, happened). If I had refused to listen to them, I would have lost two sound ideas, not to mention two checks.

5) *Browse in books that aren't meant for browsing.* Spend an hour or two thumbing through some fact book like *The World Almanac* or an encyclopedia yearbook. Those columns of dry facts and figures look pretty dull to most people, but not to a writer hunting ideas. In these volumes you will find a wealth of information, greatly condensed, on what people are doing and thinking in the world today. Any of those statistics could sow the seed of an article idea. An equally useful kind of browsing can be done in the yellow pages of any city phone book. The thousands of products and services that are offered for sale there tell much about our society and its problems and dreams.

Many of my ideas have come from phone books. Thumbing through the yellow pages once in the mid-1960s, I saw a pest-control company's ad. This item became a *True* article on the centuries-long war of man against rat. About ten years later, in 1974, a rodenticide ad in another phone book made me think it was time to take a fresh look at the same subject. This new piece sold to *Today's Health*.

6) *Mine your own experiences.* You have done and are doing many things in your life that may seem dull and routinely familiar to you, but these same things may be interesting, even fascinating, to other people who aren't living with them every day. Your problem: if something seems mundane to you, how do you alert yourself to the possibility that the world might want to read about it?

We get back to what I said before about talking to everybody in sight. Your primary purpose in all these conversations is to be a listener, but a secondary purpose is to test other people's reactions to what is in your head. If you find people asking alert, interested questions about something you've said or done, ask yourself whether you've stumbled onto a potential nonfiction idea.

I lived with a good idea for fifteen years, never seeing it, until my wife pointed it out to me. I had spent much of my spare time in those fifteen years trying to build a squirrel-proof bird feeder that really worked. One evening, after my umpteenth design had proved a failure, my wife and I spent an entertaining hour recalling all the other failures. Suddenly she said, "Why don't you preserve all this for posterity? Write an article about it!" She was right, of course. The thought had never occurred to me because squirrels and bird feeders had become too much a part of my daily life. I sold the story to *Travel & Leisure.*

2

THE KEY TO SUCCESSFUL ARTICLES

One afternoon in New York, feeling parched and lonesome after a day in the library, I dropped in on a genial magazine editor I knew and suggested a drink. That sounded good to him, but first he had to finish reading some article outlines and query letters. So I sat down to watch. And in that hour, a monumental truth about magazine articles was punched home to me. It was a truth that I'd always sensed rather than known. I'd never put it into words or articulated it as a specific rule in my own mind. But when I pondered it later and analyzed some of my past successes and failures in the light of it, I saw I could have saved myself many a frustration if I'd had the truth more clearly in view.

Clear focus

The magazine was a national periodical using nonfiction only. The man I was visiting was the managing editor. The stack of outlines and queries on his desk was the cream of that week's crop, sent up to him by junior editors and assistants. All the chaff had long since been winnowed out: all the semi-literate stuff, the letters scrawled in pencil, the weird suggestions from crackpots—and, too, all the not-quites that had failed to interest the junior editors or had been rejected for some mechanical reason such as a policy conflict. In short, that stack on the managing editor's desk represented the output of highly

15

literate people, good thinkers and good writers all. Each one of those outlines, in the opinion of a junior editor, showed promise of being developed into an article for which the magazine would cheerfully pay $750 to $2,000.

But only one got by the managing editor. To each of the others he clipped a piece of notepaper on which he scribbled "RWKN"—"Reject With Kind Note."

And when he'd finished he looked very sad. "Almost every one of these has a germ of a good idea in it somewhere," he said. "But the writer hasn't focused on the good idea. Instead, what he's given me is a big wad of information about a great big general subject."

He was still grumbling as he got up and put on his coat. "It makes you blue," he said. "A lot of these people . . ."— he waved at the stack of RWKN's—"are mighty smooth wordsmiths. I tell you, I'd love to buy from them. But they don't think their ideas down to a narrow enough focus. The stuff is all too broad, too general. They've got to learn that magazines aren't encyclopedias."

Creating reader interest

He had put it in a nutshell. In an encyclopedia you look for information under general subject headings. Beneath each heading you expect to find a general discussion that ranges through the whole length and breadth of the subject, but you don't expect to be entertained or excited or even necessarily interested. The encyclopedia editors can assume that you are reading their material because you have some need for the information—a need that existed *before* you picked up the encyclopedia. They feel little obligation to make you want to read.

But a magazine editor feels that obligation strongly. He's locked in mortal combat with competing magazines. He can't safely assume a pre-existing interest in any article subject. Each article must create that interest with its own magnetism.

The reader must be button-holed by the very title. He must feel suddenly compelled to read on, even though, a few minutes before, that particular subject was farthest from his thoughts. The article must not only give him information but must also offer to excite him, make him angry, give him a lift, solve some of his personal problems. And a broad, general discussion of a broad, general subject—encyclopedia style—can't reliably do any of that. Only a sharply focused article can be given the kind of title that will grab passersby and make them buy the magazine from a newsstand.

Individual, episode, or theme

Just what is meant by "focus"? There are almost as many kinds as there are nonfiction stories in print, but in a very broad way they can be grouped in three main categories. You can focus on an *individual*, an *episode* or a *theme*.

Take an example. Suppose you get interested in the subject of population. Will a magazine buy an article titled "Population"? Not likely. That's the encyclopedic approach. All right, narrow it a little. How about "The Threat of Overpopulation"? Still too broad. Make it narrower: "Will There Be Room for Everybody?" Not quite. Narrower: "Our Disappearing Parklands." Ah! At last we're down to a focus narrow enough to interest an editor. Some magazines might buy that story, but its chances can be vastly improved by making it narrower still.

Focus on an *individual*—a single person, organization or group. For example, tell the story of a Congressman who is fighting to save federal lands from the encroachment of civilization. Make it a good human story. Tell all about the man, why he has dedicated himself to the cause, how the fight is going. Make the reader laugh and cry with him.

Or focus on an *episode*. Make an exciting, suspense-filled narrative out of some small town's battle to prevent a park's being sold to a housing developer. Tell who won, and how.

Or on a *theme*. Get the readers up in arms by telling them how wasteful or dishonest real-estate practices are eating into their parklands. Urge them to do something about it.

In each of these three treatments, you can interweave some of your general, encyclopedic information about population growth. In fact, you *should* interweave it, to show how your story fits into the larger picture of current human events, to give your story an air of importance. But the general information becomes secondary to the specific, the narrow.

Sometimes you have to narrow and renarrow an idea many times before it pleases the man who signs the checks. Take a typical case from my own files. Back in 1957 I became fascinated, in a general kind of way, with the subject of missing persons. I wrote a query suggesting a general treatment of the subject: where missing persons go, how they're found, who hunts them. No magazine would touch it. Then I narrowed it somewhat by concentrating on runaway children. Still nobody wanted it. To narrow it still more, I focused on a theme: "Will Your Child Run Away?" No luck. Then I tried focusing on an episode, the story of a boy who ran away and how his parents got him back. One women's magazine was vaguely interested this time, but not enough so to give me a firm go-ahead. I put the idea in my file and forgot it for two years.

In 1959, while working on another story, I ran across a company called Tracers, Inc., which specialized in hunting the missing. I resurrected my idea and wrote a new query, this time focusing on this individual company. No go. I re-focused on an individual man, Tracers' president. Still nobody was interested.

I filed the idea for two more years. Meanwhile, Tracers kept sending me press releases with data on the manhunt business. Each of these releases contained a statistical summary showing the numbers of husbands, wives, children and others whom Tracers had traced. I don't know why it took me two years to see it. But finally, in 1961, I did. Husbands! I'd write a story telling why husbands run, with anecdotes about men who had spent happy years hiding on tropical islands before Tracers got them. Here was my focus at last! I immediately suggested it to *True,* a magazine for which I'd done a lot of writing and which likes strongly male-slanted stories. But *True* turned it down. It still wasn't sharp enough.

A couple of months later I was having lunch with *True's* managing editor. We were both feeling overworked that day, and we started talking about how nice it would be to disappear to some slow-paced, work-free Eden in the South Seas. I think the idea hit us simultaneously.

He said, "Say, you know . . ."

And I said, "Come to think of it . . ."

And after four years, I finally had the focus I needed. I wrote an article with a strong theme. It didn't merely describe the phenomenon of runaway husbands. It urged *True's* male readers to try it, or at least dream about it, themselves. It gave them pointers on how to disappear successfully, warned them against mistakes that could get them traced. I titled it "How to Disappear," but the editor, when he bought it, thought up a much more pungent title: "Do-It-Yourself Divorce." Under that title it appeared in *True* and later in an anthology.

In the later years of my free-lance career I got smarter, and then I spent much less time querying editors on ideas that were obviously too broad. Take another case from my files. The Westinghouse Electric Corp. has for many years sponsored an annual Science Talent Contest, in which promising high-school science students compete for scholarships and other awards. Every year when the new crop of winners was announced, a Westinghouse publicity man would take me to lunch and try to get me to write an article about the contest. The idea interested me, since I have a science-minded youngster of my own. But I knew an article titled "All About the Westinghouse Science Contest" would be received in editorial offices as enthusiastically as, say, a dead toad. The story needed a focus, a point of view, a narrowing.

Each year I would browbeat the publicity man about this, and he'd try to come up with a focus for me. It took him three years, but he did it. He showed me some statistics. Schools all over the country entered youngsters in the contest each year, he said. Thus it was unlikely that any single science teacher would produce more than one winner during his or her teaching career. But there were two teachers, one in a New York school and one in Wisconsin, whose students turned up in the winners' list consistently, year after year.

Here was my focus. I figured I could write an article that examined these two teachers, analyzed their methods, tried to come up with some conclusions about why they taught so well. Interwoven with this specific material could be some general comments about the need for good science teaching in this country in these nervous times. I queried the *American Legion Magazine,* which likes education stories. The editors liked the idea, eventually bought the article and printed it under the title, "A Tale of Two Teachers."

It isn't really hard to write a good magazine article, once you have a narrow focus clearly and sharply defined in your mind. Nor is it very hard to sell one. As an editor said when he heard I was going to write this book, "Sure, tell them I want material. Tell them I'm bleeding for it. But tell them it's got to be *sharp.*" Focused, that is.

3

TYPES OF MODERN ARTICLES

In general I'm against classifying literary works into types. It tends to make your thinking too rigid. I remember reading a book review not long ago in which the critic said he didn't like a certain book because it was "neither fish nor fowl, neither novel nor play nor essay." This seemed to me like a pretty silly reason for not liking something. Does it have to be classifiable to be good? Of course not. In fact, the effort to step out beyond standard classifications is what makes some writers famous.

In this chapter, and in others throughout the book, I'm going to be breaking things down into classifications. I do this simply to make the various aspects of article writing easier to talk about. Don't think of these classifications as rigid. If you have something in mind that doesn't seem to fit any of my classifications, don't worry about it. All that counts is whether it's good.

What follows is a quick survey of the main types of modern magazine articles. These are the types editors most often buy. They can be mixed together, of course: one type can be merged with another or several others. As a beginner, you may find it safer to stick to these main types as you cast about for ideas. As in any other field of endeavor, innovation has its risks. But if you've invented what you think is a new type of article and if you're willing to accept the innovator's extra risks, don't feel you've got to stick to the main types. The list below doesn't say what you *must* do, only what you *can* do.

Survey

This is a type of article in which you survey some field of activity—for example, an area of scientific research—and tell what's currently going on there. It's probably the hardest type of article to focus well, for the tendency is to write it like an encyclopedia article. I recently wrote a survey article for *Playboy*, for instance, on the subject of lasers. The editors wanted the article to include just about everything of interest that was going on in the field, and finding a sharp focus was hard. I focused on the youthfulness of the science (the first laser was built in 1960)—and, by harping on this theme throughout, managed to hold the article together when it was trying to go in all directions at once.

Profile

This is an "in-depth" study of some important or famous person, such as a movie star, or of some company or organization. It isn't as difficult to focus as a survey story, for the subject of a profile—person or organization—will automatically provide some kind of narrowing down. Even so, you must be careful not to let the story degenerate into a wad of random facts about the profilee. Decide what is important about this man or woman or organization, decide why the reader ought to care about this subject this year, and then shape your article around this theme and never let it come loose.

I once saw two articles about Red Skelton that had been submitted to one of the leading magazines. One, from an amateur writer, was nothing more than a big basket of facts about the actor; it read much like a long entry in *Who's Who*. The other profile, from a veteran article writer, focused on Skelton's fierce self-driving perfectionism. It omitted many facts that the amateur writer had included, but it was a compelling piece of prose. The magazine bought it.

Travelogue

Essentially this is a special kind of profile. It is a profile of a place: a country, an island, a city during fiesta time, a hideaway hotel. Travel articles are used by specialized magazines like *Holiday*; by airline and automobile company publications, such as the *Ford Times*, which want to induce people to travel; and sometimes by general magazines, such as *Esquire*. Like any article, a travelogue must be built around a focusing theme. If it isn't, it's only a chapter for a geography textbook. If it is, it's an article.

Alarmer or exposé

Essentially a type of survey article with a ready-made focusing theme, the alarmer is a story that dramatically points out something wrong. Recently, for example, women's magazines have carried many alarmers revealing dangers in the new birth control pills. Other recent alarmers have dealt with dishonesty in Congress, incompetent teachers and quack psychiatrists. The alarmer is relatively easy to write, as long as the subject is important enough—that is, as long as you don't have to strain to make readers care. But it is hard to research, since you have to dig up uncomplimentary facts about people and obviously don't get cooperation from those people. Unless you are a naturally aggressive type or unless you have some special knowledge of a field or a special passport into it (relatives or friends working there, for instance), don't tackle an alarmer until you've practiced researching other kinds of stories.

Narrative

Another relatively easy type to write, this kind of article simply tells a true story of an episode, usually in fairly straightforward chronological fashion. The episode may be historical —the story of some little-known but important sea battle, for example—or it may be something that happened this year, such as the story of a father's hunt for his missing son, which I did for *True* Magazine. A narrative usually focuses itself quite strongly. Even a bad writer can't easily un-focus it. The main challenge to the writer is in convincing the editor that the episode being treated has large enough implications to be meaningful to many readers. A favorite trick of historical narrative writers is to tell the reader that this particular sea battle was the turning point of whatever war it figured in —that, if the battle had not been won by our side, the whole outcome of the war would have been different. This trick doesn't always work too well and editors now are getting a little tired of it—but it is a good illustration of the narrative writer's attempt to relate his episode to larger events.

First-person

This kind of article is written in the first person—"I" and "me"—and relates some dramatic or revealing or inspiring experience that "I" have had. Usually such a story has some relevance to current news. That is, the experience deals with things that readers are currently concerned about. Magazines have recently published such articles as "My Worst Week in Vietnam," by a soldier, and "The Long, Long Walk," by a civil rights marcher. These are directly related to the day's newspaper headlines. Other experiences deal with what might be called social undercurrents—things that millions of people are worried about but that don't actually make news. For instance, one women's magazine now publishes a recurring feature called "A Young Mother's Story," and another has a feature called "My Problem and How I Solved It." These are first-person experiences of women battling problems that many women battle day after day: problems of children, money, husbands, and the like.

Since first-person experiences don't always happen to article writers, how does the writer get in on the deal? There are two ways. First, you can go out and deliberately make an experience happen to you. For example, you can join a civil rights march for the express purpose of writing about it later —or you can spend a night in a psychedelic night club or (as I did recently) a honeymoon hotel. You go as an observer, but you become slightly more than an observer. The "I" of the experience is you, the writer.

Or, second, you find somebody else who has had an experience, and you ask him to let you write an article about it in the first person—the "I" being him, not you. Usually such an article will carry a double by-line. It will say, "By Joe Smith, as told to (you, the writer)," or "By Joe Smith, with . . ." You and Joe Smith work out some mutually acceptable way of sharing the money, most often on a plain fifty-fifty basis.

There is another kind of first-person article, written by you with somebody else's "I" or by-line. The somebody else is somebody famous, somebody whose views on a particular subject will be worth reading about. Such an article usually gets started when you, the writer, latch onto some celebrity who happens to be passing through your town. Suppose it is a major political figure, like a governor who has national political ambitions. You go to see him, win his confidence, and say, "I can provide you with a forum from which you may express your feelings about the poverty program, Governor. It won't be much work for you, and you'll get your views spread far and wide." He's interested, asks for details. You say, "O.K. Here's how it works. You sit down with me and tell me what you want to say. I'll write it, you check it to see whether it's right, and then we'll send it to X Magazine. It will carry your by-line: 'By Governor —— ——.' The magazine will pay me for the article. We each come out a winner: you get the publicity free; I get the money."

This kind of deal is particularly attractive to candidates for political office during election years—indeed, to anybody whose position in life depends on his being known and admired by the public. The majority of articles "by" famous people are actually written by article writers working as ghosts. The trick, of course, is to hold your famous by-liner to a focus. He can't simply talk about anything that pops into his head. He must talk about some subject that people consider him expert in —something over which he has fought or argued publicly in the past, or on which his views can be considered interesting for some other reason.

Service or how-to

The service article is one that simply, and usually rather quietly, tells readers how to do something. How to save money on taxes, how to get a youngster into college, how to arrange flowers, how to pack for a family vacation. I personally consider this absolutely the hardest kind of article to write, for you must sweat to keep it from becoming boring. Some writers are experts in this field; I'm not, and I avoid service articles assiduously. Maybe you'll find you can write them well. If so, you'll be welcomed by editors of many magazines. Though the service article lacks fire and drama, it seems to attract a certain kind of reader, and this reader often buys the magazine for its service articles alone and remains loyal even when the rest of the magazine is falling apart and other readers are deserting in droves. Some magazines—for example, the so-called "shelter" magazines dealing with houses and gardening —consider this kind of reader their main pillar of support.

The typical service story is quite short. It starts by telling readers why it's important that they learn what it is setting out to teach. Then it teaches the subject in a non-teachy way.

Humor

Nothing is less funny than an awkward stab at humor, and unless you are deliberately setting out to become a humorist or have some other special interest in humor, my advice is: stay away from humor articles for the time being. Good humor writers are rare. I once heard a *Post* editor say that (judging from the evidence on his cluttered desk) there are only a dozen men and women in the whole country who can write a sustainedly funny piece of humor. Thousands of people think they can. It sometimes seems that every housewife finding a free day on her hands, every man finding himself idle on a vacation, sits down and writes a funny. Only it almost never is funny.

Humor is an art. I don't know whether it can be taught. I tend to doubt it. I certainly won't attempt to teach it. If you believe you are a humor writer, another Perelman or Benchley or Thurber, go ahead and try your markets. But if your ambition is only to be an article writer, content yourself with occasional flashes of humor within your articles. It's easy to be funny for a sentence or so—and, in fact, a touch of humor is welcome in almost any article. What isn't easy is to sustain humor over a span of several thousand words.

Magazines do not publish many humor articles, partly because they can't find many that are publishable. But when a good one comes into an editorial office, the whole office goes mad with joy. "If I could find twice as many good ones as I do," one editor told me, "I'd print twice as many." So the market exists—if you write good humor.

If you don't—well, there are lots of other article types to choose from. And the market for those not only exists, but it is a huge one.

4

QUERIES THAT SELL

Everybody likes to think his own trade is tougher than other people's—that it requires more training, more stamina, more complex skills. This is as true in the writing business as anywhere else. Whenever fiction and nonfiction writers get together, you're almost certain to hear an argument on the relative difficulties inherent in these two great branches of our profession.

"I have to gather a file full of facts before I can even look at my typewriter," protests the nonfiction man. "I have to travel, interview people, burrow in libraries. All *you* do is sit comfortably at home and write."

"Phooey," snorts the fiction writer. "All you do is report facts. What *I* have to do is create emotions, wring them out of my own head. In the time it takes you to reel off twenty pages of fact writing, I may sit and sweat over a nuance of meaning in a single paragraph."

Well, I'm a nonfiction man. I've earned my livelihood as a nonfiction free lance for the past eleven years. I've written a little fiction, just enough to get some idea of what it's like to work in that branch of the profession. And let me tell you something: I *don't* think fiction writing is easy. I *wouldn't* want to be a full-time fiction writer. I admire my friends who are and tip my hat to them for their sheer guts.

I'm happy where I am. For the magazine article writer has one enormous advantage over the fiction man—an advantage which, it seems to me, makes all the difference when you're trying to compare the two kinds of writing in terms of difficulty. The advantage is this: You have to write a fiction story before you can sell it. *But you sell an article before you write it.*

Oh, maybe an Ernest Hemingway or an F. Scott Fitzgerald can sell a fiction story before he writes it. Fitzgerald sometimes did, in fact. He'd go up to an editor of *The Saturday Evening Post* and say, "Hey, I've got a story in my head. It's about a fellow who . . ." And the editor would say, "That's great! We'll buy it!" But this could happen because Fitzgerald in those days was a big name. The editor knew two things about him: (1) He was a great writer, so the chances were the story would turn out well; and (2) even if the story wasn't so hot, merely having Fitzgerald's name on the contents page would sell magazines. But not many of us are that famous. With most fiction writers, an editor can't make any promises about buying a story until he's seen it in its completed form.

In the article business, things work differently. Partly it's a matter of tradition. Partly it is because a good editor can usually guess in advance what a proposed article will be like when finished. If he hasn't published your work before, he'll probably ask you to finish your first article before he makes any promises to buy. But after he has come to know and trust you, after you have given him reason to believe you'll produce what you say you're going to produce, he'll almost buy your articles before you write them. He'll do so on the basis of query letters.

The article writer's tool kit

The query letter is one of the article writer's most useful and most lovable tools. It takes only a few hours at most to do the basic research and writing necessary to turn out a good query. That few hours' time is virtually all the article writer risks.

I remember once having a drink in New York with a fiction-writing friend. He'd stationed himself in Hollywood, where he wrote (and still writes) TV scripts and magazine short stories. We were both feeling blue that day. He'd just had a short story rejected by the umpteenth magazine he'd submitted it to, and I'd had a similar experience with an article query that I was sending around.

"Weeks and weeks!" he moaned. "I spent weeks on that story! All those weeks—all down the drain!"

I didn't quite know what to say in reply. I felt a little foolish, in fact. I'd written my query in ten minutes.

Since the query is such an important part of the nonfiction writer's tool kit, it pays to spend a little time studying how to write a good one. What are the basic rules?

The first thing to remember is that article editors, like all editors, are busy. They spend endless hours reading manuscripts and queries. So when you sit down to write your query, keep in your mind a picture of this harried, overworked man, the editor, with his eyes red from fatigue and his system awash with coffee. Make things easy for him.

This brings us to Cardinal Rule Number One: *Keep your query short.* If it's longer than two single-spaced typewritten pages, it's too long. If it's one page, it's ideal. Don't try to impress the editor with how much you know about the subject you're querying him on. The query letter is simply a sales pitch. All you want to do is get the editor interested in the subject and convince him his readers will be interested, too. If he wants more information before giving you a go-ahead on the article, he'll ask for it. If you try to give him all the available information in the initial query and end up with a ten-page sheaf, he quite possibly won't bother reading it.

The query really needn't be more than a paragraph or two

long. The shortest query I ever wrote was a few lines long. I sent it to the managing editor of *True,* and here it is, complete:

> Dear Charlie: How about a piece on quicksand? Good male subject. *Readers' Guide* shows only a half-dozen stories on it in the past ten years. Story would tell what it is, where, how to get out of it. Also hot anecdotes, e.g., dramatic story of a college student who died in quicksand in Florida. Sources would be geology profs, New York soil-engineering company that specializes in quicksand, U.S. Geological Survey. Best regards. Max.

The editor phoned me two days later to tell me he liked the idea and to give me some instructions on how long the article ought to be, how I should organize it, where it should fit into my schedule in relation to other *True* projects I was working on. At this point, the article was, in effect, sold. Unless I goofed and turned in a bad story, I was virtually certain of getting paid in the end. Thus, from here on, I wouldn't be risking any of the time I might spend researching and writing the piece.

I wrote it. *True* wasn't happy with the first draft, so I wrote another. The editors liked this one, bought it and printed it. Eventually it was condensed in *Reader's Digest,* and still later it was condensed again for a new edition of the *Book of Knowledge.* All these were my winnings from the gambling of a few minutes' time on a query letter.

Now we come to Rule Two: Tell the editor precisely what he needs to know to make an intelligent "yes" or "no" decision on your idea. There are six elements that should be included in every query, either directly expressed or implied. If any one of the six is missing, the query isn't complete; the editor doesn't have what he needs for his decision. And if this is the case, of course, all he can do is say "no."

Six elements for a good query

Here are the six elements, in the order in which they almost always appear in a good query:

(1) If the editor doesn't know you, introduce yourself. Tell him why he should consider you a potential writer for his magazine. Keep it brief—one sentence if possible, three at most. Say what your writing experience has been, naming big-magazine credits if you have any.

In the quicksand query cited above, this element is implied rather than expressed. I'd been working with *True* many years at the time and, of course, did not need to tell the editor who I was. In writing queries to editors who don't know me, I almost always use these exact words:

> (here I mention magazines in which I've most frequently appeared in the current year). I'd like to propose an article idea to you.

That's all. Then on to the next element:

(2) State what your idea is in a nutshell—in one sentence if you can, in one paragraph at most. Sometimes this is easy. In the quicksand theory, Element No. 2 was neatly taken care of by the simple little sentence, "How about a piece on quicksand?" More complex ideas may take longer to put in nutshells. For example, I once wrote a query to the editor of *American Legion Magazine* in which my Element No. 2 read like this:

> This idea has to do with a new, experimental way to handle high-school dropouts. Several cities, among them New York and St. Louis, have worked out a kind of work-study plan in which kids go to school part of the week, put in time at paying jobs the rest of the week. In terms of the youngsters' morale and a re-awakened desire to stay in school, results have been remarkable.

In both the quicksand query and the dropout query, this Element No. 2 served the function of telling the editor exactly what the proposed article was going to be about.

(3) Tell the editor briefly (in a query, everything is "briefly") what his competitors have been doing about this or related subjects. He's got to be convinced that other, competing magazines haven't run the same story—or, if it's a popular, newsy subject, that your particular approach to it is different from anything yet printed.

I always check back through the past ten years in *Readers' Guide to Periodical Literature* before writing a query. If I find my proposed subject has been covered in many publications, and if my approach is not radically different, I don't write the query. It would be a waste of time. But if the subject has been but sparsely covered, this fact becomes part of the query's sales pitch. Note the third sentence in my quicksand query, carefully telling the editor that this is not an old, overused, worn-out idea. Hardly anything makes article editors madder than to be queried on subjects their competitors have long since milked dry.

(4) This element can come either before or after Element No. 3, depending on how the words seem to flow best. In the quicksand query, it comes before. You tell the editor why he should be interested in your idea, why his readers should be interested, why he should care.

Don't make it into a door-to-door salesman's pitch. Don't exaggerate. Don't use Madison Avenue phraseology: "an irresistible idea; a must; will draw readers like flies." This will only irritate the editor. Simply state the facts in the idea's favor, calmly and quietly. In the quicksand query I got by with three words for my Element No. 4: "Good male subject." No amount of embroidery with purple adjectives could have made this little sales talk any stronger.

In my dropout query I managed to weave Elements 3 and 4 together like this:

The problem of school dropouts has been the subject of much discussion lately, in print and on TV. Kids leave school, dump themselves on the labor market and discover that this increasingly complex, technological society has no use for their meager skills. It will be refreshing to report that there is a potential solution to this huge problem—a solution that won't cost taxpayers a cent. The story of this solution hasn't yet been told anywhere except in local newspapers of the cities concerned.

(5) Now supply a few more details about how you propose to write the story, what it will contain, what it will say. In effect, what you are doing here is expanding on what you have said in Element No. 2. Give a sample anecdote, a case history, a statistic or two, a few of the story's key facts. If it seems necessary to help the editor envision the proposed article, give a sketchy plan of its framework.

This element is likely to be the longest section of your query. But don't let it run away with you. The temptation will be strong, here more than anywhere else in the query, to snow the editor with the wealth of your knowledge. You'll want to tell him every good anecdote, every juicy statistic. Don't. Tell him just enough to show him the article is possible, the materials for its structure are at hand, the architecture will be attractive.

In the quicksand query, I contented myself with listing a few of the elements that would make up the story and then with sketching a fragmentary anecdote. In the dropout query, I gave a few statistics dealing with the school histories of kids who had and hadn't been through the work-study experiments, and I briefly told the story of one boy who had learned the value of education by working at a paying job. What the editor got in each case was an advertisement something like one of those "Coming Attractions" blurbs in the movies: a quick glimpse of a few compelling scenes.

(6) Finally, answer questions that may be in the editor's

mind about the mechanical details of your proposed project. Tell him what your sources of information are going to be. If you happen to know of some good illustration possibilities for your story, tell the editor about them. If you're querying on some hot news subject that will be dead by next year, explain to the editor what your proposed schedule will be and when you plan to get the article finished.

And that's all there is to it. Assuming your proposed article idea is a good one, a query written like this will get attention.

What really matters

Your query can be in informal language, like my quicksand one. It can be more formal, like my dropout query. It can be in a rigidly engineered outline form, with heads and subheads. It can be set up as a letter to a specific editor (all of mine are, for no really good reason), or it can be a general query addressed to nobody in particular, capable of going from one magazine to another without retyping. It can be single-spaced or double-spaced, on your letterhead or on plain paper, folded like a letter or shipped flat. None of this matters much. All that really matters is what the query says.

In your early years as an article writer, editors won't usually react to your queries with direct, flat promises to buy the proposed articles. Instead, when an editor likes the sound of your query, he'll reply in hedged language. He'll say, "Your idea interests us, and we'd certainly like to see the article when finished. But, of course, we can't make any guarantees . . ." Or he'll say, "This sounds like a possible article, and if you want to write it on speculation we'll be happy to read it . . ."

Don't be discouraged by this equivocal language. Remember that you're unknown to the editor. He would be very foolish to do more than give you this mild encouragement. How does he know you'll turn out a printable story? All he can do is hope—and his equivocal letter represents that hope.

But his hope should be enough to spur you to action. Out of

every hundred queries he gets, ninety-nine are rejected with a plain and unequivocal "No, thanks." When an editor expresses even faint hope for an article, it means that he wants to see the article printed in his magazine. He will work with the writer to make the article viable.

So go ahead and write your article even though the editor has not guaranteed to buy it. If the article is what the query said it would be, if it lives up to your query's promises, chances are the editor will be happy with it. If there's something wrong with it, he'll send it back to you with instructions for revision. Eventually, with a minimum of luck, you'll sell it to him.

PART TWO

 Research

5

DOING RESEARCH BY MAIL

There are four main ways in which a nonfiction writer gets the facts he needs to build magazine articles. He does his research (1) by going to sources of information in person, (2) by telephone, (3) by mail, and (4) in libraries. The relative importance of each method is dictated partly by the personal preferences of the individual writer, partly by the requirements of the individual story. But often, too, it is dictated by circumstance. Often a writer doesn't have all four methods available to him.

This is particularly true of the part-time free lance—the man or woman who works at something else all day, writes only at night or at other odd hours chopped out of a busy week. I free-lance full time now, but I remember how it was when I was a part-timer, holding a nine-to-five job and struggling to write articles after supper. Method One was not always feasible for me: I couldn't leave town for a whole day or several days to travel about the country, as I do now. I couldn't casually hop aboard a plane and fly a thousand miles to interview somebody. My employer was a reasonable man, but not *that* reasonable. Method Two, the telephone, was a little easier, but as a beginner I had no real assurance that I'd ever be paid for what I was writing; nor did I have any editor's promise that he would reimburse me for my expenses. Thus I could not too frequently pick up the phone, as I do now, and call someone across the country to ask for information. This left me with Methods Three and Four as my major means of article research. Method Four, the library, is useful as a way of picking up background information. By definition, a library isn't a source of new, never-before-published information—and this of course is the kind of information that magazine article editors buy. Thus the beginning or part-time article writer's best way of getting new facts is Method Three, the U.S. Mail.

This restriction made me restless and irritable when I was beginning. I wanted to travel, I wanted to grab the phone and call Peru. Maybe you feel similarly confined. But listen: the restriction isn't nearly as harsh as it may seem. Used properly, the mail is one of the nonfiction writer's most valuable tools. A good information-asking letter—a *good* one—can often accomplish as much as a personal interview or a phone call, sometimes more. I still use the mail liberally, even though I can travel and telephone at will. Some full-time free lances I know use the mail more than any other research method. One of them, in fact, uses the mail almost exclusively. He's a painfully shy man who is scared stiff of telephones and hates airplanes. Yet, getting most of his data by mail—operating under self-imposed restrictions exactly like those of the part-timer—he has become a top magazine free lance.

I've seen some of his information-asking letters. They're good—and that's why they get results for him. If you're depending on the mail to furnish you with the factual bricks and mortar for your articles, your letters need to be good, too. If they aren't—and it's surprising how many writers' letters aren't—you might as well go out of business.

I nearly went out of business myself in the beginning. Once I mailed out a hundred letters and got three mediocre replies. I thought: "I'm doing something very, very wrong. If I can't average better than this, I can't write articles for a living." As time went by, I began to see some of the things I was doing wrong, and little by little my average got better. Some years ago, seeking data for an article on the island-selling business, I sent out seventy-five letters and got forty-three replies, most of them exactly the kinds of replies I'd hoped for. At last, I figured, I knew what I was doing.

Ten rules

I'm still learning, of course. Human beings are infinite in their variety, and a letter that might produce a good reply from one man might end in another man's wastebasket. Still, I think I know some of the main rules by now. There are ten that I consider, in general, the most important:

(1) Always send any information-asking letter to an *individual man or woman,* not to a company or other organization. Sometimes this is easy and obvious. If you're writing a medical article, and you hear of a doctor who has invented a new kind of operation, and you want details, obviously you send your letter to that doctor. But suppose (to take a recent example of my own) you want some nationwide statistics on automobile theft. You figure the FBI may have what you want. Do you address your letter simply "FBI, Washington"? Not if you want it answered, you don't. A letter addressed that way will be opened by mail clerks, will drift around the huge organization for a while and eventually, probably, get lost. Even if it does land on the right man's desk, he won't feel urgently compelled to reply. He'll know *you* don't know he has your letter. The situation will be so impersonal that he simply won't be motivated to act.

No, you've got to send a letter to a specified individual. In the automobile-theft case, I addressed my letter to the FBI chief himself, Mr. J. Edgar Hoover. A reply containing precisely what I wanted came back in a few days.

(2) Send the letter to an *interested* source. Ask yourself: "Who will want to give me this information? Who will profit by giving it?" In the FBI case, it was easy. Mr. Hoover was

known to be concerned about his relationship with the press and often went out of his way to be good to reporters. I knew he'd want to help me.

But suppose you're writing to an organization in which you don't know anybody's name. A letter addressed simply to "The President" or "The Director" will often get results. Much faster results can usually be had by addressing "The Public Relations Director." Almost every moderate-sized organization in the country has somebody called either the Public Relations, Publicity or Public Information Director (it doesn't matter which title you use; he'll get your letter), and it is his job to get his organization favorably mentioned in the press. He'll *want* to help you. You'll find such a man in nearly every industrial company, hospital, college, research institute, foundation, military installation, U.S. and state government bureau, city police department.

If there's no public relations director to help you, you've got to think a little harder about who will want to give information. Once, working on a major magazine piece on school integration, I wrote to the principals of two schools in a town that was having racial troubles. Neither man replied—and, when I thought about it, I could see why. The principals were caught in the middle of a messy situation; and no matter what they said, somebody was bound to get mad at them. Obviously, then, they wouldn't want to talk to a magazine reporter. So I wrote two more letters: one to a lawyer who was representing a group of Negro parents, the other to a lawyer representing white parents. Each of these men (and I should have seen this in the first place) wanted his own side of the argument publicized. Each sent me a huge amount of information and opinion.

(3) Use pleasant, friendly, informal language. Make the man *like* you. It's amazing how many professional writers—of all people—forget all they've learned about the English language when they sit down to write a letter. Their letters are cold, stuffy, stilted—like a letter from a lawyer. Don't feel you must

adopt commercialese just because you're writing to a company president, or stand at attention because you're writing to an admiral. This man gets enough stiff letters during his day. Relax. Use contractions liberally—"I'm" instead of "I am." Joke with the man if the occasion seems to warrant it.

One of the most pleasant exchanges of letters I ever had began when I wrote to the director of the U.S. Fish & Wildlife Service with a question about duck hunting. My letter contained some silly but irresistible pun—something about "fowl play," as I recall. The director's assistant wrote back with a better pun of his own, I wrote back with another to top his, and he replied with a whole horrendous series. In the process, I got all the information I needed.

(4) Explain precisely why you need this information. Don't just ask a question and let it go at that: "Dear Sir, Please tell me how many tons of steel your company produced last year." Explain that you're a writer, you're putting together an article for such-and-such a publication, the article is about this-and-that, and you need the information for such-and-such a purpose. Nobody likes to be asked a question in the dark. Would you like it if somebody telephoned you and said, "Good morning. How often do you brush your teeth?" Of course not. You'd want to know who the devil this caller was and why he wanted to know about you.

(5) Capitalize on your status as a member of the press, in a position to offer free publicity. Point out (subtly) that you can put before the public this man's or organization's name, achievements, opinions. I often do this simply by asking, toward the end of the letter: "May I have permission to quote you by name?" I know I don't need to ask the man's permission, and he probably knows I know—but when he sees the question, it brings home to him the fact that he's going to see his name in print. It will be hard for him to resist replying.

Another way to accomplish the same purpose is to state, in an offhand way, the circulation of the magazine you're writing for. I usually do this with some such phrase as, "I'm sure *True*'s two and one-half million readers will be interested to know . . ." In other words, what I'm not-so-subtly telling the man is, "Reply to my letter and I'll give you an audience of two and one-half million."

(6) Make your request for information sound important, so that the recipient himself feels important. Make him think he's the only man in the whole world who can track down this needed data for you. Even if you're sending the same letter to a hundred people, don't tell any one of them about the other ninety-nine. Never use any such phrase as, "You're one of fifty people whose opinions I want to get . . ." Never send out mimeographed form letters or questionnaires, unless you're prepared to be satisfied with a two percent return. Do everything to make the recipient feel that he, and he alone, can lead you to the end of your arduous research trail.

(7) Ask only specific questions—only the kind that call for short, quick answers. Never ask a man a question that will require an essay in reply. He probably won't reply at all, for you're asking too much. In my school integration research, for instance, I was tempted to write to everybody involved and say, "Please give me your opinions on school integration" —for this, basically, was the stuff of which my article was to be made. But the question was too general, too vague, too *huge*. What I did was to break it up into six smaller, specific questions: "Do you believe that the integration of schools will help solve other racial problems in your town? Do you think the children themselves are ready for integration, even though adults may not be?"—and so forth. Each question could be answered by a simple yes or no, if the respondent so chose. But, as it turned out, few respondents could resist the urge to hedge, modify or otherwise comment on their replies—and some, in fact, wrote essays.

Sometimes you do need to ask somebody for a huge amount of information. Recently, for example, the New York *Times* asked me to do an article ("humorous and affectionate," the editor said) on the New Haven Railroad, a commuter line in the New York area on the brink of bankruptcy. I needed to know everything about the railroad: its history, financial status, miles of track—everything. Yet, I knew it would be senseless to write to the railroad's Public Relations Director and say, "Please send me all available information on your railroad." The request would simply buffalo the man. What I did, again, was to break it up. I asked for specified kinds of literature: "Is there a booklet or press release that tells the New Haven's history? Can you also send a copy of the latest annual report. . . ?" This way, the man knew exactly what I wanted. And, being an intelligent man, he judged from reading my letter that I might be able to use a few extra items that I hadn't asked for. He sent a thick sheaf of material. With a few personal interviews and a short ride on the railroad's bar car, my article was researched.

(8) If your subject is a ticklish or controversial one, offer to let the man read and blue-pencil the manuscript (or those parts in which he's quoted) before you send it to the editor. This is the only way to handle explosive subjects by mail. You won't get many replies otherwise. People may be willing to talk to you face-to-face about birth control or racial strife, but they often hesitate to put down their thoughts in a letter. A letter, stark black and white, often takes on the aura of a legal document in cases like this, and people are afraid to approach their pens and typewriters. You have to put them at ease.

(9) Make your letter seem urgent. Give it a faintly breathless sound, as though you've got to have a reply tomorrow or the whole world will fall apart. People are busy and lazy, and will endlessly put off answering a letter if the letter has a casual feeling. I often send my letters Special Delivery, simply to startle the recipient, make him feel this is no ordinary letter. (The extra cost isn't great.) And, toward the end of the letter, I always make a mention of deadlines. "My dead-

line on this article is rather close," I tell the man, "so may I hear from you as soon as it's convenient?"

(10) Make it a habit to write and thank every respondent for his reply, and be sure to file away either his letter or his name and address so you'll be able to find it next year. In short, once you've found a good source of information-by-mail, hang onto him. You never know when you'll need him again. There are literally scores of men and women all over the country who have given me data or opinions for more than one article each. I've never met them and I don't know what they look like or sound like, but they and I are good buddies.

Letter writing

One man in particular, a man named Reuben Kidd living in Sacramento, California, is perhaps my best proof of the value of careful letter-writing. I live near New York, so we're a whole country apart. I first learned of him back in the late 1950's, when I was writing an article on divorce for *True*. In a library newspaper file I read about a Mr. Kidd who had organized a group dedicated to reforming the nation's divorce laws. I found his address by going to the telephone company and looking him up in the Sacramento phone book. I wrote to him. He wrote back with information. Since then, I've had occasion to ask his help with three other articles on related subjects. He always replies with great bundles of data. I always thank him.

We've never met, but by now we're excellent friends. He's Reuben to me, I'm Max to him. He knows how I think, I know how he thinks. I can ask him complex questions in a few words because he knows, from past contact, the kinds of articles I write and the kinds of fact and opinion I seek.

I really don't think I'd get more dope out of Reuben if I flew to California and interviewed him in person. That would cost hundreds of dollars. As it stands, all I have to do is buy a stamp.

6

RESEARCHING IN LIBRARIES

If there is any single person in the world whom you should strive to make your friend, that person is your local librarian. The library may not be big and may lack most of the books you want to consult, but the librarian will be a key figure in your professional life. He or she (usually she) can tell you about books other than those in her own library, can suggest sources of information you would never have thought of by yourself. Usually she'll know about other libraries in your region and will know, or have some quick means of finding out, whether these libraries contain the volumes you want. Make it a point to introduce yourself to her and tell her you write for magazines. She will be pleased to be called on for help. Much of her day's work is pretty humdrum, and she may find your research problems quite stimulating. You may be surprised at the amount of work she will be willing to do for you.

If you live in a small town or suburb, as I do, you'll probably find yourself visiting your local library often, and occasionally visiting a big library in some nearby city or university town. I do all the work I can in my local library. It is small, I know all its rooms and cul-de-sacs, and I can usually find any volume within minutes. It would take half an hour to get hold of the same volume in the New York Public Library, so it makes sense always to try the little library first. Over a two-week span I make a list of volumes I need that are

47

not available locally, and eventually I take this list to the big city and spend a day burrowing in the enormous bookery at 5th Avenue and 42nd Street.

Starting point

The library will usually be your starting place for article research. Whenever you get an article idea, or whenever an editor assigns you a subject, your first step should be to go through the latest volumes of the *Readers' Guide to Periodical Literature*. This valuable publication lists by subject matter every article published each month by most major magazines (with a few odd but notable omissions). Comb through it to find what other article writers have done with your subject in the past five or ten years. Take down the names and issue dates of the magazines, and then go to the nearest big library that keeps a magazine file and read all the articles.

In these articles you will find a lot of information about your subject. You'll also get the names of people to whom you can go for more information—people whom all those other writers have quoted or named as experts on the subject. In most cases, you will find not only the expert's name but also some clue as to where you can get in touch with him. For example, the previous article writer may have used some such phrase as, "According to Dr. Henry Jones, psychiatrist at XYZ University Hospital. . . ." All you need to do then is find out what city XYZ University is in (by looking it up in the *World Almanac,* for instance), and you can write Dr. Henry Jones an information-please letter.

When Dr. Henry Jones writes back to you, he may suggest other sources, name other men who are experts in your subject. Thus you will have developed sources of your own—and this is what you should strive to do. Use the previous writers' articles only as a starting point.

The *Readers' Guide* is probably the publication most often consulted by article writers. But there are others almost as important, and it will pay you well to make friends with them. Here's a list of them and what article writers use them for:

Phone books. Most big libraries have fairly complete collections of American phone books. If you are not near such a library, your local phone company has such a collection. To find a man's address when you know only what city he lives in, consult the phone book of that city. To get a list of companies that are in a certain line of business, or men who are in a certain profession, check phone listings in the classified or "yellow pages." (The yellow pages are also a good source of article ideas, incidentally. When you run dry of ideas, go through a thick classified telephone directory and glance at some of the odd services and professions that are listed.)

Who's Who. There are many kinds of *Who's Who,* some dealing with prominent people in general, some limited to a single category—such as commerce and industry, education, music. If you want to get in touch with some fairly prominent man or woman but don't know how, the *Who's Who* volumes will usually give you a home town and often a street address as well, plus other tidbits of information, such as the person's age and birthplace.

Thomas' Register of Manufacturers and the *Standard & Poor's Directories*. These list business firms, phone numbers and addresses; tell what the firms do; give names of top executives.

Encyclopedias. Use these circumspectly, especially if the set is an old one. The information is likely to be badly out of date. To an article writer, the main value of an encyclopedia lies in two areas. First, it can give you general background data on facts that do not change from year to year. (If you want to know the land area of Kansas, consult an encyclopedia. If you want to know the population of Kansas, don't consult an encyclopedia, consult an almanac.) Second, it can lead you to sources. Many encyclopedia articles carry the writers' by-lines, and somewhere at the back or front of the set you will find a listing of each author's credentials, usually including some clues to help you find him. Write him a letter and ask what's new in his field since he wrote the encyclopedia article. At the end of an article, too, you will often find a bibliography, a list of reference books, and other published material on the subject. Read this material, track down the writers and ask them for up-to-date information in the same way.

Statistical Abstract of the United States. An enormously useful book published annually by the U.S. government, containing statistical data of the kind that can give an article weight and body. If you are writing your articles properly, they are sharply focused on a single individual, episode, or theme—but they should also include material that will show readers how your focal subject relates to larger and more general phenomena. The *Statistical Abstract* will give you such material. If you are writing an article about divorce, for instance, you might focus on an individual divorced woman and her problems. To show what her problems mean to the country in general, you go to the *Statistical Abstract* and get figures on how many divorcées there are in the United States, what their average income is, whether there are more or fewer of them than ten years ago, what their statistical chances are of remarrying, and so on.

The World Almanac, Information Please Almanac, Reader's Digest Almanac and similar books. These are published annually, and you should use them to get the kind of constantly changing data that you can't get from an encyclopedia. You can also use them effectively to find sources. For example, *The World Almanac* contains a long list of associations and professional societies. If you are doing an article about some aspect of circuses, to pick a subject at random, you go to this list and see if there is any kind of society in the field. It turns out there is an outfit called the Circus Fans Association of America, and its address is given. You write to its director or executive secretary and ask your questions.

As you gain experience in using libraries, you will no doubt make friends with a lot of other books. Every article writer has his personal favorites. The ones I have listed are favorites of almost every writer in the business.

When you quote

A word about the question of giving credit. If you use a phrase, sentence or paragraph verbatim from any published source and put it in your article, you must put the material in quotes and fully identify the source. This needn't be done in a formal or stilted way, as long as the names of the writer and publication appear. For example: "Joe Smith wrote last year in the *XYZ Review* that there are 'seven times as many brown-eyed pink mice in Mississippi as pink-eyed brown mice.'"

If you simply use a fact from a published source without quoting verbatim, you must use your judgment about whether or not to give credit. In general, it is a rule-of-thumb that you must give credit for a "proprietary" fact but need not give it for a "common" fact. A proprietary fact is one that a writer has dug up through original research; it appears in his book or article but cannot be found anywhere else. A common fact is one that appears in many publications—for example, the land area of Kansas or the atomic number of silver. Usually you can sense quite quickly whether a fact is or isn't proprietary. When in doubt, give credit. You can't get into any trouble by giving credit where it isn't due, but you can get into a lot of trouble by failing to give it where it *is* due.

Background and sources

And one final word of caution. A modern magazine article should not contain more than a few scattered quotes from published material. It is ten times better to quote what a man has *said* than what he has *written*. If an article gives the impression that it has been built mainly from published sources, the editor will say, "Well, if it was all written somewhere else before, why should I bother publishing it again? There can't be anything new about it." So, in general, use the library only for background information and for digging out sources. If you find some published material that says what you want to say in your article, try to avoid the temptation to quote directly from that publication. Instead, send a letter to the man who wrote it and ask him to say the same thing to you in different words. Ask him questions that will elicit the words you want. When you get a letter back from him, quote from the letter: "Dr. Jones says," instead of "Dr. Jones once wrote . . ." It sounds new, much livelier, much more fresh, much more interesting.

7

CONDUCTING A SUCCESSFUL INTERVIEW

No matter how effective your information-by-mail operation may be, there is bound to come a time when you must seek information by talking to somebody. It is virtually unavoidable. Magazine articles are principally about people, and you cannot operate for long as an article writer without interviewing men and women.

It won't be the President of the United States, maybe, or a movie star, or anybody rich and famous. That will come later in your article writing career, if it comes at all—and even then it won't happen often. Most of the people you talk to will be obscure and humble—the corner druggist, a local doctor, the town clerk. Even so, you may feel shy about approaching them. You may think you are imposing upon them. Perhaps you are basically a shy person to begin with—a fact which you think will make matters still worse. As a young man once expressed it to me, "I love writing, and I particularly love writing nonfiction. What scares me is the time I'll have to spend away from my typewriter. I don't meet people easily. I'm a writer, not a reporter."

I told him two things. The first was that a nonfiction writer, at least one who hopes to write magazine articles, has to make up his mind that he's going to be a reporter as well as a word-smith. The second was that becoming a reporter is really the very easiest part of becoming an article writer.

Asking questions

I was shy too, in my early days. I got along well enough with people, but I was really worried about my ability to ask questions in the right way. I had seen movies (as you probably have, too) about brave, brash newspaper reporters who seemed totally unembarrassed about asking the most personal kinds of questions under the most difficult circumstances. I thought, "Where do they get the nerve? Can I ever be that kind of reporter? And if not, can I ever be an article writer?"

I remember well the first major free-lance assignment I ever tackled. It was for *The Saturday Evening Post,* back in the early fifties. I had suggested an idea for a story on a household appraiser, one of those people who estimate the value of a home and its contents for inheritance or estate-tax purposes. All the editors liked the idea basically, but warned me that they would not buy the story if it contained what they called "too much sweetness and light." One of the editors wrote to me: "We imagine that not everybody loves a household appraiser; for instance, in situations where the appraiser puts a high value on a home and this results in a high estate tax. We imagine that an appraiser gets into arguments, is sometimes called nasty names, is accused of making mistakes, and maybe does, in fact, make mistakes. All this, if it squares with the facts, should appear in your proposed story. We envision the story as having a bittersweet tone."

This scared me. It meant, I thought, that I'd have to ask nasty, nosy questions, like one of those reporters in the movies. Did I have the guts?

It turned out I didn't need them. The appraiser I chose as my focal character was a charming elderly lady named Jenny Schreiner. I phoned her, told her who I was and what I wanted, made an appointment and went to visit her in her apartment. Tucked into my pocket was a list of questions nice and nasty. She ushered me into her sitting room, gave me a cup of coffee and started to talk about herself and her profession. She talked and talked. She was so flattered to think that any magazine might be interested in her that she laid bare her entire life for me. Almost without my saying a word, without my asking a single direct question, she answered every question on my list, plus a number of others that it had never occurred to me to ask. She seemed to sense that I didn't want to hear only nice things about her, and told me the bad as well as the good. She gave me everything I wanted, and the editors bought the article immediately.

I'd had visions of her getting angry at me, throwing me out of her apartment. Instead, we became such good friends that Jenny Schreiner later had dinner with my wife and me.

The point is that people aren't as hard on reporters as the beginner may fear. Most people are flattered to be asked questions. Nine out of ten enjoy talking about themselves, their lives, their occupations. They enjoy it even in casual conversation. When they think that they may see their names in print, they enjoy it all the more. Nine out of ten, too, have that innate modesty or sense of balance, or whatever you wish to call it, that precludes their telling you only the admirable facts about themselves. Most will tell you of their mistakes and setbacks. They'll tell jokes on themselves. They'll invite you to laugh with them.

Techniques and devices

It's up to you to get them started, however, to get them moving in the direction you want to go. There are almost as many reporting techniques as there are article writers, and you will almost certainly develop your own after your first two or three interviews. But here are some major points of interviewing technique to keep in mind:

1. Except in unusual situations where you must act very fast, always write or phone for an appointment beforehand. Even if you plan to interview the subject by phone, call him up first and ask him to set a date and hour some time in the future when he can conveniently talk to you. Then phone him back at that exact hour.

There are two good reasons for doing this. The first is one of common politeness: you can't barge in on somebody, either in person or by phone, and reasonably expect him to drop whatever he was doing and spend half an hour or more with you. The second reason has to do with the nature of human thought. When you first approach your man and tell him what you want to interview him about, he may have trouble collecting his thoughts on the subject. He may be surprised at the sudden prospect of getting his name in a magazine (most people are), and he may be bewildered and perhaps even a little frightened. By setting the interview a day or two into the future, you give him time to calm down. He mulls over the subject, recalls facts that he probably would not have remembered if you had interviewed him more suddenly, maybe even goes through books or papers dealing with your subject matter. He's anxious to give you what you want, and by allowing him a little time you enable him to do so.

I remember phoning a doctor once during the preliminary stages of research for an article for a leading magazine on child suicide. I didn't know where to go for information, and my approach was to call directors of psychiatric hospitals and ask them to suggest likely sources. When I first talked to this man and told him what I wanted, he was very pessimistic. "Well, you're welcome to come and see me," he said, "but I really don't think I'll be able to help you much." I told him I'd like to see him anyway and made a date. When I turned up in his office after a three-day wait, he was beaming with success. During the three days, he had talked to other doctors and had collected a whole list of sources for me—people around the country who were doing research on child suicide or were otherwise knowledgeable about it. What's more, he had even done some of my library work for me. He handed me a sheet of paper listing references to medical journals in which cases of child suicide had been written up. None of this could have happened if I'd phoned him and tried to interview him on the spot.

2. In your preliminary phone call or letter, be sure to introduce yourself completely and tell the man or woman precisely what you want to talk about and why. Leave no mystification in his mind. On the phone, I usually use some such phraseology as this: "My name is Max Gunther. I'm a magazine writer, and I'm writing an article for X Magazine on such-and-such. I thought maybe you could help me."

At this point the man usually mumbles politely that he'll do his best, but there is still mystification in his tone. So I next go into details. I tell him more specifically what the article is about. I tell him precisely what aspect of the subject I want to talk to him about. And I tell him where I got his name and what made me think he could be helpful. If I do it right, he is no longer mystified. He now knows what his relationship is to this stranger on the phone, sees the situation, and understands how he fits in. If he doesn't understand all this clearly, he will be reluctant to submit to an interview.

3. Let the person you are interviewing do all the talking he wants to do. I usually show up for an interview with a short list of prepared questions, but these are only for emergency use. If the man or woman is balky, afraid to talk, or simply shy, then I go down my list of questions one by one. But nine out of ten people will talk of their own accord once you get them started. As long as they don't stray too far from your article subject, all you need to do then is sit and listen. If you continually interrupt such a flow of words by injecting pre-

pared questions, you may lose a lot of good anecdotal material and "color"—or you may make the interviewee clam up altogether.

One of the most difficult interviewing assignments I ever tackled grew out of that child-suicide article I wrote. I had to interview the parents of a six-year-old boy who had attempted suicide twice. The object of the interview was to get emotional rather than factual material: I wanted to know what the parents *felt*, not so much what they *did*. They were reluctant to talk to me in the first place, and I knew this was going to be a toughie. I prepared a list of about twenty questions and prayed I wouldn't have to use them. The only real chance of getting what I wanted, I knew, lay in somehow making the distraught man and woman open up and tell the story in their own way.

So I opened the interview with a single question which, I hoped, would make them see me as a fellow human being rather than a nosy reporter. I asked the question sincerely, because I really wanted to know the answer: "Before we begin," I said, "tell me just one thing. Is your boy all right now?"

That did it. Now we were three worried adults, not two interviewees and a reporter. The father said, "Well, we think he's O.K., but—you see, it's hard to tell with him. He was always a little hard to fathom." And the mother said, "Yes, right at the beginning we noticed strange little quirks . . ." And they were launched on their story. They talked to me for two hours. I barely asked another question the whole time. They told me their deepest feelings in a way that would never have been brought out by direct questions. ("Were you upset?" I'd have asked. "Yes," they would have said. And what good would that have done for my article?)

4. Try to keep the entire interview friendly and informal—even if you must ask for information the man doesn't want to give. The more it resembles a casual chat, and the less it resembles a formal interview, the better your results will be.

One of the worst interviews I ever saw conducted took place at a scientific convention in New York. A girl reporter and I both wanted to interview the same scientist about the same subject, and to save his time we arranged to talk to him together. We met him in his hotel room. The girl had a big looseleaf notebook which seemed to scare him right away. It looked so prominent, so formal. When we sat down, she took from her handbag four newly-sharpened pencils and laid them in a neat row on the coffee table. I could almost hear the scientist's worried train of thought: "Oh-oh, I've got to be careful about what I say." It was almost as though he was being made to testify in a courtroom. As he began to speak, I saw to my horror that the girl was taking down his every word in shorthand. Every now and then she'd hold up her hand and say, "Wait! You're going too fast! Let me catch up!" The scientist became so tense that he ended by saying almost nothing at all.

The next morning I happened to see him eating breakfast in the hotel dining room. I wandered over to his table with my coffee, sat down and talked to him informally, with no notebook. He answered every question he had failed to answer the day before.

The casual approach

Sometimes, a person will talk most freely and colorfully when he thinks the formal part of the session is over. Once, doing a piece on the complicated subject of lasers, I had to interview an Army weapons research officer in Washington, D.C. It was a hard interview because he didn't want to answer any questions at all. I'd ask, "Is the Army considering the use of lasers as military weapons?" And he'd look pained and say, "Afraid I can't comment on that." His public information officer was sitting by his side like a watchdog, nodding in agreement at every "no comment." The interview seemed to be failing completely.

Then, through the open door, I saw a man go by pushing a coffee wagon. I said, "I can use some coffee. Will you join me?" They thought that would be a fine idea—for, like me, they'd been finding the interview painful. I closed my notebook with a loud and pointed snap, pocketed my pen, and stood up. The interview was over.

As we drank our coffee, we talked casually and laughed at the humor of our situation and wondered how long it would be before the Army would allow its officers to talk freely about lasers. The weapons research officer said, "You know, there are some things we're doing that I really wish I could tell you about." And, without actually giving away any classified data, he told me about them. In a cab on the way back to my hotel, I took out my notebook again and wrote down everything I could remember of what he'd said.

Some article writers go still further than that in the attempt to establish an informal atmosphere. One man I know avoids interviewing people in their offices. He meets them in less formal situations: over meals, traveling somewhere, fishing. One of his best interviews, he once told me, took place while the person he was interviewing was raking leaves on his lawn.

I never use a tape recorder simply because it tends to make the person interviewed nervous, puts him on notice that every word he says may be used against him. Sometimes I don't even use a notebook. I just sit slouched in a chair and listen, and nod. The object is to get the interviewee relaxed, to make him really *talk* instead of just answering questions.

PART THREE

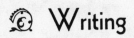 Writing

8

BUILDING THE FRAMEWORK
OF AN ARTICLE

About fifteen years ago, it was possible to sell a type of magazine article that some editors called the "string-of-pearls," and some called the "tell-me-a-story story," and some called the "Old Curiosity Shop." I think "string-of-pearls" describes it best. When beginning writers ask me how magazine articles are organized or structured, I always start by talking about the string-of-pearls article. Every beginner in this field should study the string-of-pearls style with care, for at least three very good reasons:

1) As far as I know, no major magazine editor has bought such an article for at least a decade—nor seems likely to buy one ever again.

2) This is exactly the type of article many beginners try to sell.

3) By studying this obsolete style and understanding why it is obsolete and what has replaced it, you'll begin to see how a modern magazine article should be constructed.

A typical example of the string-of-pearls appeared in a now defunct magazine some 25 years ago. I don't know why this particular article sticks in my mind, for there were thousands upon thousands like it. At any rate, it serves as an illustration. Its title was "Golf Cutups." In his lead section, the writer established his subject matter. He said, in effect, "Lots of

famous people have done lots of funny things on golf courses."
The rest of the article was nothing but a string of stories about
famous people's high jinks on the links.

This is the kind of article that magazine editors sought in
the first half of the twentieth century. The article's parts—its
anecdotes, facts, curiosities and bric-a-brac—could be presented in virtually any order, just as equal-sized pearls can be
strung in any order. The rationale for including any given part,
its reason for being there, was simply that it had some vague
relevance to the subject matter established in the lead. The
main challenge to the writer was that of effecting smooth,
quick transitions from part to part; and back in those days,
the writers who could "transish" (as they called it) best were
the writers who sold the most stories. At least one big-name
writer of my acquaintance used to construct his successful
articles (all for top magazines) by writing the parts on separate
pieces of paper, spreading them out on his office floor and
then shuffling them around until they were in some pleasing
kind of order. Finally, he'd transish them together—and lo,
he'd have a finished article. It made smooth reading, but it had
no real framework, no more than does a string of pearls.

Theme, point, conclusion

Beginners submit literally hundreds of such articles, outlines, and queries to big magazines every week. Somehow, it's
characteristic of beginners—and even more so of non-writers
—to believe that this outdated kind of non-story is good magazine material. At least once a month some non-writer comes
up to me and suggests such an article drawn from his own
experiences. Last time, it was a lady who works in a plush
women's hat store. "You wouldn't believe all the crazy things
that happen in a hat store!" she told me. "I bet you could
write a terrific article about it!" I mumbled polite agreement.
But I knew my chances of selling any such non-story were
slim.

A good magazine article today must have a solid framework. It must have a theme, make a point of some kind, drive toward a conclusion. It must have a tight-knit feeling. Like a short story, an article must have a discernible beginning, middle and end. It must lift the reader up, carry him along and set him down with a satisfying thump—and he must end with a strong sense of having arrived somewhere, of being in a different place from the place where he started. Obviously, if an article is so loosely built that its parts can be rearranged in almost any order, there is little hope of making the reader feel he is going anywhere.

These concepts—tight-knit feeling, feeling of going somewhere—are partly subjective and, as such, hard to talk about. Perhaps a simpler way of focusing on the same concepts is to say that a modern magazine article should set out *to prove something*. It shouldn't amble up to the reader with the bland invitation, "Read this, it's interesting." It should stride up to him and grab him by the lapels and shout, "See here, I'm going to tell you something important, and you've got to believe it!" The body of the article, instead of just reeling off a string of curiosities about golf cutups or hat shops, will now be a structure of logic and emotion that (you hope) proves what you said you'd prove. It *has* to be such a structure; you're obligated to make it so because that's what you've promised the reader. Thus, by the simple act of setting out to prove something, you almost automatically begin to build a framework for your article.

Consider an example from my files. Back in 1965 I opened a long and, for a while, fruitless dialogue with the editors of *Playboy* Magazine. We were something like fiancées who couldn't agree on a date and place for the wedding. *Playboy* pays well and is a likable magazine; I wanted to write for it, and the editors wanted me to write for them. The editors and I were agreed that a good subject for me to start with would be the "Science of Sound," a piece dealing with supersonics, city noise problems and other related material. But for about a year and a half I wrote not a word of it. Neither the editors nor I could figure out a way to make the story jell. As originally conceived, it was just a string-of-pearls—unwritable for me, unpublishable for the magazine. As one editor put it, "The title of this story could be, 'All Max Gunther Knows about Sound.' Just a big bag of facts. It wouldn't *go* anyplace."

Well, all through 1966 that unborn story kept nagging at me. I'd take out my file of clippings and riffle through them, and mope, and put the file away and turn to other, viable ideas. Once in a while I'd phone some company in the acoustics business to see whether any new interesting facts had developed. And one day an acoustical engineer told me: "You know, the science of acoustics has existed for hundreds of years, but nobody ever paid any attention to it before. Now, suddenly, everybody is interested. We're almost getting to be glamour boys like the atomic scientists!"

A bell in my head clanged loudly. At last the piece was coming to life! The article would set out to prove what the engineer had said: that this long-neglected science had become a space-age darling. This would be the framework upon which I would hang my "big bag of facts." This would be the theme that would give the article life and movement, the underlying structure that would hold it knit together. I wrote the article. *Playboy* bought it instantly, and it appeared in the May 1967 issue—precisely two years after the editors and I first started to negotiate.

Design and structure

Once you've decided what your article's underlying theme will be, what it is meant to prove, the actual designing of the framework becomes an almost mechanical process. You fix in your mind the thing you are trying to prove. You consider the parts you have available to construct the proof—and, of course, if the parts on hand don't stand up to the job, you either go out and get what's missing or you abandon the project. With the research completed, the parts all ready for use, you put them together in such a way that they carry the reader logically, step by step, to your conclusion.

There is no single way to build such a framework, of course, just as there is no single formula for fiction and no single architecture for a house. Yet any good house, however architectured, has its own compelling logic. Its parts belong in *this* order, not in any random order. *This* beam rests on *that* wall; *this* timber accepts *that* stress. Just as an illustration, here is the way I constructed my framework for the science-of-sound article:

1) The *lead:* something to clutch the reader hard and fast, convince him immediately that he should care about sound. I used a dramatic description of military experiments in the use of sound as a weapon.

2) *Transition* out of lead: a statement of subject matter, a promise to the reader that I'm going to prove something to him. I tell him, in effect: "I told you that story about sonic weapons because I want to show you that sound is now an 'in' science. I'm going to prove it to you by telling you about some fantastic new developments—and you'd better care, pal, because sound is part of your life and could one day be part of your death."

3) Now a more leisurely *restatement of the theme:* I tell about the old days, when acoustics scientists were ignored or laughed at. Plenty of specific examples. Then I say, "But times change."

4) The pace quickens again as I move into a *"flash-by"* section: dozens of one-sentence glimpses of the newly-glamorized sound business. Sonic gadgets, sonic experiments. The examples are specific and concrete; companies and individuals are named and fully identified. I imply that the reader may phone these people himself, if he likes, to verify my statements. The reader is an intelligent man, and I know he won't accept

my words about the sound business unless I give him these specific illustrations. I'm still laboring to prove what I said I'd prove—and the need to do so is still shaping my framework.

5) The pace slows to a walk now. I tell the reader, "Before you can understand this material fully, you've got to know something about the basic physics of sound." I give him a short, almost textbook-ish *lesson* on the subject. I figure he'll stay with me because I've already given him a lot of startling material, and I've promised more to come. But I don't make him sit still for more than three typewritten pages.

6) Then on with my *proof:* an expansion of Section 4, the flash-by section. In greater detail and with plenty of anecdotes and quotes, I give examples of new sonic gadgets and experiments. I return briefly to the lead material and give more examples of military experiments, again carefully naming names so the reader will know I didn't make all this up. Again and again, but never repeating the same words, I reiterate the single theme, the thing I'm trying to prove. I never let the reader forget it. I want him to be starkly aware of the framework at all times. I want him to know where I'm taking him, feel himself going there. This is by far the longest section of the article—and might, I suppose, be called the "body" or "main trunk." But I'm careful to make it drive toward the conclusion. Toward the end of this section I want the reader to feel himself running faster and faster downhill, and I deliberately make the sentences shorter, the style more jittery. Finally the reader slides (if I've done it right, hurtles) off the end of this section and splashes into . . .

7) The *conclusion*. It isn't a climax, actually. "Climax" is too strong a word. It's more like a coda, a brief finishing statement. In this case it's a two-paragraph anecdote that illustrates what I hope I've now proved. It's as fast and short as I can make it. It contains no reiteration, no summing-up. It

simply tells its illustrative story, makes its point and shuts up. The article is ended.

Promise and proof

Recently I wandered through my house and gathered every current issue of every magazine my wife and I subscribe to—fourteen in all. They contained about eighty articles all told, and I read each with care. This is an exercise I prescribe for myself once or twice a year. Usually I'm interested in finding out what subject matter other writers have tackled, but this time I was equally interested in story structure. All but two or three of the articles (those were offbeat types for which there are no rules) exhibited a structure substantially like the one I've outlined.

I don't mean every article had seven sections like my science-of-sound piece. I mean each had a structure that arose logically from the writer's promise to prove something. Each was like a well-built house, with one part resting solidly on another. Each had a nice up-and-down movement, with slow material following fast material and a definite *downhill* feeling toward the end.

There were several articles with a "chronological" structure, for example, and these had essentially only four main sections. One that I remember particularly, because it was so well handled, had a title something like "How We Cured Our Drug-Addicted Son." It was a mother's first-person account, perhaps ghost-written by a professional article writer. The mother began with a long, dramatic anecdote—a detailed description of the day when she first learned her son was hooked on drugs. Then she paused to state her theme and make her promise of proof. She told me, the reader: "I'm going to prove that warm family love can help pull an addict away from drug dependency." Then she plunged fast into her third section, a chronological account of the family's three-year struggle. This was the long "trunk" section, but it had its own internal up-and-down movement. Just when it seemed to be overdoing the drama or verging on the sticky-sweet, it paused briefly for a paragraph of dry humor. It sped downhill to its conclusion, which was a short, simple and moving anecdote illustrating the boy's revulsion against drugs and his sudden wish to help others kick the habit.

It was a well-framed story. It was no string-of-pearls. Reading a string-of-pearls, you could stop in the middle if your eyes were tired or something else claimed your attention. This one wouldn't let you stop. I didn't stop. The editor who originally read it didn't stop either, obviously. He paid the writer the ultimate compliment. He bought the story.

9

RAISING THE CURTAIN: LEADS

Once long ago, when I was working on *Time* Magazine, the writer who shared my cubbyhole office was assigned an unusually long and difficult story. He was given four days in which to write it. At the end of three days he hadn't written a word. He'd spent his time staring at the blank sheet of yellow paper in his typewriter, or reading newspapers down to the last obit, or morosely prowling the corridors, or dragging me out into the streets of New York for meals, snacks, drinks, walks and coffee. I was worried. "Look, buddy," I kept telling him, "you'd better get cracking." He could only shrug helplessly.

Finally, late on the third night, his typewriter suddenly started clacking. I looked up from my own machine, and there he was—going like mad! He'd solved his problem at last, whatever the problem was. He was on his way!

But a little while later he was standing up, reaching for his coat. "Well, I've made it," he said with an air of huge relief. "I'm going home."

I looked at his typewriter. He'd written only half a page. He must have seen my frown, for he grinned. "Listen," he said, "when you've got the lead, you've got the story licked."

Yes, he had it licked. He'd spent three days composing his first two paragraphs, but he needed only one day more to finish the job—and a fine job it turned out to be.

The first few hundred words of a magazine article are, indeed, hard to write. But they always reward the effort of writing them well, and that's why my *Time* buddy ceased to fret as soon as he'd squeezed that reluctant lead from his brain. He knew he had a good lead. And he was confident that, with this much accomplished, the rest of the story would almost write itself.

Angle, focus, aim

What is a good lead? It's one that does two things well:

First, it grabs the reader hard. It makes him want to read on. It's like the poster outside a theater or movie house: it lures the customers in.

Second, it accurately points out the direction the article is going to take. It aims straight at a target—namely, the end of the article. It establishes the *flow* of the article, and, having grabbed the reader, plunks him into this flow so that he can feel himself going somewhere.

A lead must do both of these jobs. If it doesn't, chances are the article won't come off. Obviously, if the lead doesn't grab the reader (or the editor) in the first place, the rest of the article simply doesn't get read. Not so obviously, if the lead doesn't establish a definite flow in a definite direction, the reader will either lose interest or become confused and irritated. He has to feel himself traveling down some intellectual or emotional river toward an unseen but sensed destination.

A good lead not only holds the reader; it helps the writer. Once you have your article well aimed, it will flow from your typewriter without huge effort. You'll know where you're going. And once you have your reader securely captured, you can confidently take him through abstruse, complex, textbookish, or other heavy material without fearing you'll lose him. You won't have to strain constantly to hold him, risking all the attendant dangers of over-dramatization and cuteness.

Before you can write a good lead, obviously, you must know

exactly what your article will be trying to say—not only the general subject but the focus, the thing to be proved, the conclusions to be drawn. If you don't have these elements firmly fixed in your mind, you can no more write a lead than you can shoot an arrow at a target while blindfolded. Some writers outline or do a rough draft of their articles first, then write their leads as part of the final polishing step. Others prefer to map out an article mentally beforehand, then write the lead, then let the rest of the article flow out of the lead. This second way has always seemed to me to be by far the most effective, though the preliminary mental mapping-out is often agonizing. Before sitting down to write the lead of any major article, I usually spend at least a day—sometimes a week—ambling disconsolately about, mentally nudging the article's component parts around until they fit together in some pleasing, sharply defined shape.

Three basic types

Once you know what your article will be driving at, the next step is to decide on the type of lead that can launch it best. There are basically three types of lead, each with its special uses:

1. *The anecdotal lead.* This chapter starts with such a lead. It's a story of a single individual and serves to illustrate some of the general statements made later on. This kind of lead grabs the reader in much the same way and for the same reasons as does a work of fiction: it is a story about a human being with a problem. Generally speaking, this is the easiest kind of lead to write and—probably for that reason—the most popular among nonfiction writers.

The anecdotal lead is particularly useful for articles without a great deal of dramatic content or fiction-style storytelling. The lead serves to lift the article off the ground, make it feel less like a piece of required reading in a school textbook.

2. *The statement lead.* You use this kind of lead in cases

where you have something startling or unusual to say, something that can be said joltingly in your first few sentences. For instance, I once wrote an article for *True* on "weather warfare"—attempts by Russia and the United States to learn how to control weather for military purposes. In the course of research, I ran into a government scientist who theorized that a prolonged drought on our East Coast and a recent increase in Midwestern tornadoes might be results of enemy weather-tampering. Here was my obvious lead:

> Something strange is going on. Maybe you've noticed. The weather has gone haywire. It has changed drastically—not only here but all around the world.

I then gave a few examples of drastic climatic changes, and from there rolled into a high-voltage, italicized sentence that served as both a punch line for the lead and a transition into the body of the article:

> *Is somebody changing the weather deliberately?*

In another case, *This Week* Magazine asked me to write a tongue-in-cheek statistical study of American Presidents—how many were six feet tall, how many were farmers' sons, and so on. I fretted for two weeks before I saw my lead for this one. I wanted an anecdotal lead at first, but no anecdote seemed able to express the half-joking, half-serious frame of mind in which the editor and I wanted readers to approach the article. Finally I hit upon a statement lead that did the job perfectly:

> President Kennedy started life all wrong by being born in May. No boy born in May had ever before made the White House.

You should *not* use a statement lead in any case where the statement is flat or unsurprising. Scrabbling through my attic the other day, I came across an article I'd written for my grade-school paper decades ago. The article, potentially a pretty good one, was about unusual summer vacation trips enjoyed by my classmates. It started with what may be the worst lead ever written:

Many persons leave town for their summer vacations.

3. *The prose-poetry lead*—often referred to as the "purple" or "novelist's" lead. This is the hardest kind to write, the least likely to come off successfully. You use it as a novelist would use it: to establish a mood, draw the reader into a certain way of looking at things or feeling about things. I used this kind of lead once for an astronomy article for *The Saturday Evening Post*. A *Post* editor had taken me to lunch several years ago, and told me he wanted an article describing man's expanding knowledge of the universe. The assignment sounded impossible. How could I compress so huge a subject into 5,000 words? I worried about it for more than a year before finding the courage to start writing. I tried and discarded over twenty leads. All of them sounded too "small," incompatible with the massive scope and sweep of the subject matter. Finally I decided that the only way to get the article off the ground was to use prose-poetry, a patch of purple that told of my own emotions:

In a near-infinity of burning stars and black space so enormous that it absolutely cannot be imagined, on a speck of rock so small that to mention it seems almost ridiculous, tiny creatures called men are trying to find out where they are.

This seemed to do the job. It told the reader what the article was going to be about, gave him an emotional viewpoint.

Variation and combination

These three basic types of lead are capable of endless variation and combination. If you wanted to write a textbook about leads, you could probably find several hundred sub-types.

There's the "You-Are-There" anecdote, for instance, in which you ask the reader to imagine that he himself is in a certain situation, faced by a certain problem. (For example, I once wrote this lead for an article on automobile safety: "You're driving down the highway. It's a bright, sunny day. Ahead of you, a car signals a left turn . . .") There's the multi-anecdote or string-of-pearls lead, in which you tell several short, quick, one-paragraph stories and follow with a transitional sentence: "These stories illustrate an important and baffling problem . . ." There's the biographical poem: "Joe Smith is a big man, not handsome, not ugly . . ." It isn't really necessary to know the type and sub-type of every lead you write, the way a biologist classifies insects, but it's overwhelmingly important to know what each lead is trying to accomplish, and how, and why.

While deciding on the type of lead that will best launch your article, you must also decide what the lead is going to say. If you ever took a journalism course you probably learned that a good newspaper lead tells the reader "who did what, when and where." The first paragraph of a newspaper article tells the whole story in a nutshell, so that the editor can print the first paragraph alone if he's hard up for space. Magazine articles are never cut that much, and for this reason a magazine writer can be more leisurely about stating his subject matter. But don't take too long. By the time the editor has digested your title and your first two manuscript pages, he should know precisely what the article is going to be about. The chapter you're reading now begins with a five-paragraph anecdote, and the sixth paragraph (beginning "The first few hundred words . . .") states the subject matter and viewpoint, and makes the transition into the body of the chapter. A lead should never be much longer than that.

A newspaper story almost never stops to tell the reader *why* he should bother reading it. Newspaper reporters and editors start with the assumption that their readers have a pre-existing wish to know the day's news. But in writing a magazine article, you can't make any such convenient assumption. You have to tell the reader, either directly or by inference, why he should care about your subject. You must tell him this in your lead.

In this particular chapter I didn't need to bear down too heavily on this element. This is a book for writers, and I could assume that most readers would come to the chapter with a pre-existing interest in my subject. All the same, the second sentence of my transitional paragraph tells you why I want you to care about leads: ". . . they always reward the effort of writing them well."

In most general magazine articles, you've got to come down a little more heavily. For instance, in my *This Week* article about Presidents, I used the third paragraph to remind the reader that his own son was potential Presidential material, and that by reading my article he could arm himself with facts to help gauge the boy's chances of making the White House. I said it jokingly, yes—but I made sure the reader thought of the article as bearing on *himself*, through his son.

It is almost impossible to overdo this "why-you-should-care" theme in your lead. It's a key part of the reader-grabbing process. Even if you think you've laid it on too thick, the editor may lay it on still thicker. I once wrote a story for *Good Housekeeping* about office romances—situations in which a married man falls in love with his secretary or a working wife with her boss. It seemed to me that *Good Housekeeping*'s women readers would find obvious relevance to themselves in the subject, and I didn't do much about telling them why they should care. The editors shot the article back to me and asked for a "strong paragraph" pointing out that no wife really knows what her husband does all day, that the most faithful of husbands may meet temptation sometimes, etc., etc. I wrote the paragraph, thinking it a little too heavy. When the article appeared in the magazine, the editors had made it still heavier.

Not only that, but they'd rewritten my title to reinforce this "why-care" theme. "When to Worry about an Office Romance," shouted the 36-point purple print. And underneath, in hot pink: "How ominous are the words, 'I'll be working late'?"

News pegs

Sometimes the "why-care" element is part of another element called a "news peg." A news peg is a sentence or paragraph referring to some recent important news event or series of events, and establishing your article's relevance to that news. Essentially it's an excuse that you and the editor make to the reader, explaining why you're presenting him with this article now instead of next year or last year. For instance, I once wrote a story for *True* Magazine about electric batteries. This was in 1965, and my news peg was the massive electric-power failure that paralyzed the northeastern United States one November night that year. I opened with an anecdotal lead, a story set in New York City where flashlight batteries sold for $2 apiece that wild night. This served the double purpose of connecting my article with current news and demonstrating the importance of batteries in an emergency.

The news peg can be much more general than that, referring to some current news *topic* instead of one specific event. For instance, in an *American Legion Magazine* article on high school science teaching I handled my why-care paragraph like this:

> This problem, vital in any age and any advancing nation, has been the focus of special worry in the United States over the past decade. With Soviet Russia turning out scientists on a mass-production basis . . .

Once you've got your reader well hooked and thoroughly immersed in the flow of your article, the rest is easy. Well, comparatively.

10

USING ANECDOTES

A lot of business offices have corny signs hanging on the walls. They say "Think" and "Genius at Work" and other bits of nonsense. The typical writer, respecting words and their meanings, hangs no such signs in his office because they only irritate him. Yet there is a sign that I'd like to see hanging before the eyes of every beginning article writer, a first commandment of article writing. It consists of only two words: BE SPECIFIC.

If there is a single flaw more common to beginners in nonfiction writing than any other, it is the failure to be specific. The tendency to make general statements without supporting them, without illustrating them; the tendency to write a magazine article like an encyclopedia article will result in failure.

In a previous chapter we examined one way of being specific: the technique of bringing an article down to a sharp focus, narrowing its subject matter so as to concentrate attention on one specific part of a broad, general field. In this chapter and the next, we shall look at the two principal ways of being specific *within the body* of the article: anecdotes and quotes.

Can it stand alone?

Suppose I come up to you and say, "Magazine offices are crazy places." That's a general statement. Not very interesting in the first place—and, just as bad, not wholly believable. But suppose I say, instead, "Last week at X Magazine, a free-lance writer got so mad at an editor that he clobbered the editor on the head with a rolled-up manuscript, then threw the manuscript out the window." That's an anecdote—a specific illustration of the general statement that magazine offices are crazy places. It is both more interesting and more believable than the general statement.

And notice this: when you've read the anecdote, and *only* then, the general statement becomes worthy of being taken seriously. The anecdote can stand alone; it makes its point, and the reader can infer the generality from it if he wishes to. But the general statement cannot stand alone. The general *must* be supported by the specific.

In actual practice, you can write an anecdote before, after or without a general statement. In the chapter on leads, "Raising the Curtain," we looked at the common anecdotal lead, in which you tell a story and follow it with a general paragraph that says in a broad way what the anecdote was saying in a specific way. Here's another example of the anecdote-followed-by-generality structure. It is from a story I wrote for *True* on vacation homes. I was trying to make the point that there is a huge and growing demand for hideaway homes, and that homebuilders and prefab manufacturers have awakened to the demand and begun making money from it. I did it like this:

Vermont farmers looked up into a bright blue sky one day last year and saw a . . . *what?* The farmers blinked and looked again. Yes, that's what it was: a house, drifting lazily through the air beneath a large helicopter. A fully assembled house: walls, floor, roof, even curtains in the windows. It was being hauled to the ski slopes on top of rugged Mount Ellen.

This was the anecdote, the *specific* statement. What followed was the *general* statement, introduced by a short transition sentence:

The farmers may have thought this was just another tom-fool notion of those crazy danged ski folks from the cities. It was, indeed, an unusual sight. But the thinking behind it was neither unusual nor crazy. That house floating over the hills was a prophetic comment on a wild, fast-rising new phenomenon of the American scene. Quite suddenly, millions of Americans have decided they want hideaways in the wilderness. Just as suddenly, builders and building-materials makers have begun catering to this booming market with zeal and imagination. A house small enough and light enough to be lifted by helicopter . . .

And so on. Note that the anecdote serves the two purposes of making a general statement believable and making the point in an interesting way. Suppose I had contented myself with the general statement alone and simply started with this sentence: "Quite suddenly, millions of Americans . . ." It would have been flat, dry, not memorable. And there would be no reason for readers to believe it, for I would have offered them no proof. Later on in the article, of course, I offer statistical proof of the statement. But by using an anecdote, I give them an immediate demonstration—solid, tangible evidence—that my general statement is not hogwash.

Reversing the order, you can write the generality first and then illustrate it with an anecdote. The most common way to do this is to use the "for example" locution: "Tigers are dangerous. For example, once when I was in the jungle . . ." But any phrase like "for example" gets tiresome if it's repeated too often. So you must search for other ways to word it. Here's an illustration from another *True* article of mine on the subject of franchise businesses. Halfway through the article I made a general statement and proved it with an anecdote like this:

You can make money as a franchise-holder. You can even get rich. A lot of men are glad they once answered a franchising company's ad—men who, but for that lucky circumstance, might still be trapped in obscure jobs with no hope of ever making a big buck.

Art de Felice, for one. Art was a resident of Brooklyn, New York. He was 26 years old . . .

Then I went ahead with the story of how Art de Felice got rich. Note again that the general statement, without its supporting anecdote, is pure hot air. Only the specific story about the individual man makes it worthy of belief.

Anecdotal material is so strong that it can even be made to stand by itself, with no associated generalities whatever. You do this most often in the conclusion of an article. In fact, it is one of the best ways of ringing down the curtain. If you have an anecdote that very clearly illustrates what the article has been saying, or makes an important final point within itself, you can simply plunk it down at the end of the article with no transition and no generalities to introduce it.

I did this, for example, in that piece I mentioned earlier on child suicide. The subject was a gloomy and macabre one, and I felt the need to inject a note of optimism at the end. I wanted the reader to finish on the upbeat. So, right in the middle of some gloomy statistical material, I engineered an instant change of pace and smacked the reader with a surprise anecdote, without preamble, without generalities or transition. The preceding material had been talking about child suicide rates in various foreign countries, and this is how the anecdote came onstage:

. . . the countries with the lowest child suicide rates are Norway, England, Italy and Belgium. (Russia and China don't usually release vital statistics, so little is known about their suicide problems.)

Dr. Harry Bakwin, a New York pediatrician, was once called to treat a 5½-year-old boy who had jumped out of a seventh-floor window. He was stuporous for five days, but by incredible luck had done no lasting damage except to break some bones in one foot. Probing the youngster's history, Dr. Bakwin found—hardly believing it—that for at least two years he apparently had been obsessed by the idea of suicide. He had tried to kill himself again and again:

by jumping from windows, banging his head against walls, jumping in front of cars.

The causes of his distress were hard to fathom. But whatever the causes were, they seemed to go away by themselves as he grew up. At the age of 8½ he was still having problems: he was a troublemaker in school and was doing poorly in most of his courses. But he hadn't made a suicide attempt in three years.

A doctor asked him what he would ask if granted three magic wishes. His answers showed that he now shared some typical American dreams. His first wish was to be famous, his second to have lots of money. His third wish was to live forever.

And that was the end of the article. I allowed the reader to draw his own generalities from the specific. It would have been silly for me to end this hard, compact little story with a generalizing statement of my own: "And so, dear reader, as you can see, there's always room for hope." This would only have weakened the impact. No: the anecdote needed no support. It stood by itself, made its own point, carried its generalities within itself. The best thing for me to do when I'd written it was to stop.

The split anecdote technique

There's a rather uncommon fourth way to handle an anecdote, and this is to insert your generalizing statement right in the middle of it. Uncommon—but, in certain situations, very useful. You do this most often when the anecdote is a long one and you fear that the reader may be getting lost, possibly be wondering what point you are trying to make. As we've noted before, you must never allow this to happen to the reader. He must always feel himself going somewhere in some definite direction. He must never stop, puzzled, and ask, "Why is the writer telling me this?" If he does that, you've lost him. The split-anecdote technique helps you guard against this possibility. Just when the reader is getting fidgety, wondering why

you are telling this long story, you pause and tell him why—
and then you go on with the story.

I did this in the lead anecdote of a *True* article on cryogenics,
the science of extreme cold. It began like this:

> The man on the operating table was in serious trouble. His
> body was tense and rigid. His arm shook with continual
> rhythmic movements that he was powerless to stop . . .

It went on to say that the man was afflicted with a nervous
disorder called Parkinson's disease. Then I continued:

> Bending over him were Dr. Irving Cooper and staff mem-
> bers of St. Barnabas Hospital in New York City. A strange
> instrument was in Dr. Cooper's hand . . .

I explained that the instrument was a special kind of needle
or probe whose tip could be made intensely cold. By this time,
I realized, the anecdote was running long. It had already
covered two long paragraphs. The reader (assuming he hadn't
read the title, which readers sometimes don't) would be wondering what the article was about. Was it about Parkinson's
disease? Operating rooms? The life and times of Dr. Cooper?
I felt it was time I pointed out the article's direction, told the
reader where I was taking him. So I paused in the middle of
the anecdote:

> Dr. Cooper was about to demonstrate one use of the
> science called cryogenics, the science of extreme cold. It's
> a relatively new science—but it's one that has created some
> remarkable developments over the past few years, and some
> strange wild hopes for the future. Medical men like Dr.
> Cooper are particularly fascinated by the possibilities.

Then I went on with my story about the man with Parkinson's disease, telling in detail how Dr. Cooper used the super-
cold probe to destroy a malfunctioning part of the man's brain.

Having made my general statement and established the article's subject matter in the middle of the lead anecdote, I could now let the case history run as long as it wanted without mystifying the reader.

Making the general credible

Since part of an anecdote's job is to make a general statement credible, it's desperately important that the anecdote itself be credible. By far the best way to make an anecdote sound true is to identify people and places by name. In the cryogenics anecdote, for instance, I identified a man (Dr. Cooper) and his place of work (St. Barnabas Hospital, New York). This has the effect of proving to the reader that I didn't invent the anecdote. By naming man and place, I tell the reader, in effect: "If you don't believe this story is true, go ahead and check it out for yourself. Call Cooper at St. Barnabas and ask him to verify what I've said." Now, obviously, the typical reader is not going to make any such call. But by tacitly inviting him to do so, I make my anecdote entirely credible.

Thus, whenever it's possible, you should pin down every anecdote with real names of real people, places, organizations. Include all the information a reader might need to track down the people and verify your truthfulness. Don't just say "Dr. Irving Cooper, an East Coast surgeon." Don't just say "a doctor at St. Barnabas Hospital in New York." Neither of these identifications is complete. Include everything but the man's phone number.

"Blind" anecdotes

Sometimes, of course, you can't identify real people by name. This happens particularly when the article deals with some delicate personal subject. People you want to interview on the subject will tell you, "O.K. I'll give you my story, but you must promise not to use my name in your article." In cases like this, you'll have to use what are sometimes called "blind" anecdotes —anecdotes in which the characters or places are not named. Even so, you must include at least some identifying information so that the anecdote does not sound wholly fictitious. Perhaps you can include the city where the anecdote took place, or the name of a company in which the main character is employed. There must always be *something* to tie the anecdote down to reality.

In a New York *Times* article on alimony, for instance, I used an anecdote about a woman whom I identified as "an attractive Manhattan divorcee in her mid-forties." The reader doesn't have enough information with which to telephone her and verify the story, but at least I've told him she lives in Manhattan. That's better than nothing. Similarly, in a *True* article on divorce and alimony, I identified a man as "a young businessman now serving time in New York's infamous Alimony Jail." I did not name the man, but at least I named the place where he was to be found.

No article should ever be built preponderantly of blind anecdotes. Use too many, and you invite charges of writing fiction. My personal rule is never to use two blind anecdotes in a row, but always to put at least one fully identified anecdote between them. An identified anecdote has the effect of lending credence to the blind anecdote that follows. The reader says to himself, "Well, the writer *could* have made up this story in which nobody is named. But since he named real people and places in the story just before it, I guess I can assume he's telling me the truth."

Another way of lending credence to a blind anecdote is to name the source. For instance, in a *Playboy* article about electronic computers, I wanted to tell an anecdote about a company that used a computer inefficiently and ended by losing a lot of money. This story would have been embarrassing to many people if I'd identified the company—and in fact, since elements of dishonesty were involved in the anecdote, I could have ended in court as the defendant in a libel suit. So I didn't want to identify anybody. The anecdote had to be blind. How could I make it believable? By telling the reader where I'd heard the story. I began the anecdote by saying, "Computer scientists at Honeywell, Inc., tell the story of . . ." The reader might not be willing to believe me, a mere writer; but I figured he'd probably be willing to believe what a big company said.

You'll find many blind anecdotes in the pages of magazines. In almost all cases, at least in the higher-paying magazines, you'll notice that the writer has done his best to make the anecdote credible by giving just as much identifying information as he could. Yet, as a writer yourself, you may have a question to ask: Are all these anecdotes as true as their authors have tried to make them sound? Or are some of them pure fiction? Can an article writer sometimes make up an anecdote when he needs one?

The ring of truth

That's a good question. It is obvious that blind anecdotes *can* be made up, and almost equally obvious that some article writers do it. Editors are aware of this, and some editors care and some editors do not. Whether you make anecdotes up or not is largely a matter of personal choice.

But if you want my advice, don't.

I ask forgiveness for moralizing, but in the first place it has never seemed proper, to me, to cheat your reader. A magazine presents him with two kinds of reading: fiction and nonfiction, each quite clearly labeled. The reader trusts the magazine, and his trust ought to be repaid. If you present him with something that you have labeled "article," it should not contain fiction.

But enough moralizing. There are two other good reasons, hard pragmatic ones, for avoiding fictitious anecdotes in an article. The first reason is that a fictitious anecdote can backfire on you with quite painful results. An editor might ask you,

"Just out of curiosity, who *was* that guy in your anecdote about the Alimony Jail? Where did you get his story?" And if you've invented the anecdote, what are you going to say to the editor? Are you going to admit that you lied in print, in the hallowed pages of his magazine? Maybe the editor will think it is all a good joke, maybe he'll even admire your yarn-spinning skills. On the other hand, maybe he won't. Maybe he'll suggest that you never waste time submitting stories to him again.

The second reason for sticking to factual anecdotes is that the act of writing disguised fiction can make you lazy. You will discover that it's easier to make up an anecdote than to get up out of your chair, go out among people and talk and read and listen. And as your articles grow progressively more fictitious, they will lose the ring of truth.

It's hard to say exactly what the ring of truth is. It is something you sense (and an editor senses). A good article has it, a bad article doesn't. You'll find lots of bad articles, for instance, in those grubby sex-and-sensation magazines: articles that are quite obviously pure fiction throughout. Their writers obviously haven't stirred from their chairs or even picked up a phone or written a letter in search of facts.

Sure, their way of writing articles is easy. But look at it this way. They get paid perhaps $25 per article. For a *good* article you can get anywhere from several hundred to four thousand dollars.

To me, that seems to make the extra work worthwhile.

11

THE USE OF QUOTES

A quote serves the same purposes as an anecdote, and does so only slightly less strongly. It is a way of being specific, a way of backing up general statements, a way of putting sparkle into what might otherwise be dull material. The ability to use quotes well will be one of your valued tools as an article writer.

A quote is essentially repeating what somebody has said, usually in his own words. You can quote directly: "I am ninety years old," says Henry Smith. Or indirectly: Henry Smith says he's ninety years old. Either way, properly done, the quote adds a certain kind of zing to your prose.

Borrowed credentials

People use quotes all the time in ordinary conversation. Most often they use quotes as a way of adding authority to their words. One woman might say to another, "My doctor tells me it's dangerous to drink a lot of coffee after you're forty." An indirect quote. Why did the woman use it? Because she knows her own theories about what you should drink are not authoritative or indeed interesting to anybody else. But her doctor's opinions are presumably based on sound training and real knowledge—and, hence, are worth listening to. In effect, the woman borrows her doctor's credentials in order to give her own words more weight. You do the same thing in a magazine article. You support your generalizations by quoting an authority such as a doctor.

You can use quotes effectively in any part of a magazine article: beginning, middle or end. In a *Popular Science* article on the subject of letter-writing, for example, I led with quotes like this:

> Samuel Johnson, cantankerous 18th Century lexicographer, listened morosely one day while a merchant complained about the amount of letter-writing required in his business. "It strikes me as unfair," the merchant said, "that I, a merchant, must know how to write, while you, a writer, need know nothing of commerce."
>
> "Sir," bellowed Johnson, "you may be a king or a chimney-sweep, but if you cannot write, you are nobody!"

The quotes got my article off to a strong start. I used old Sam Johnson's words to tell the reader why he ought to read the article. If I'd used my own words instead, the lead would have been flat and general:

> Though writers don't need to know much about business, businessmen need to know how to write. Everybody should know how to write, no matter what his occupation.

Ghastly, isn't it? No such generalizing, sermonizing lead would please any editor of any magazine worth writing for. But by putting the same sermon into the form of quotes, by setting up a scene in which two men have a brief argument, by giving a little glimpse of old Sam's personality through use of the words "cantankerous" and "bellowed," I was able to give the sermon life and bounce and punch.

In the same kind of way, a quote can bring an article to a strong, satisfying close. Thirty or forty years ago, it was common for a magazine article to end with a summary in the writer's own words: "And now we've seen how important it is to write good letters . . ." Today, because our reading and thinking habits have changed, this has a flat and fatuous sound. It sounds as though the writer is simply trying to fill up space with words, though he has nothing left to say. There are many better ways to end an article. The conclusion need not be a summary—but if some kind of summarizing statement seems appropriate, try to put it in the form of a quote. Ideally, the man or woman quoted should be someone who has previously been introduced in the article, someone whom you've already established as an authority whose words on this particular subject are worthy of consideration.

For example, in an article I once wrote about suburban crime, I ended with a quote by a suburban police officer. I had already quoted him several times in the body of the article—and, in fact, had led off with a scene in which he was driving around at night in a patrol car. Thus the reader knew who he was, knew why I considered him somebody to listen to. The article ended like this:

"Let's face it," says Officer George Krueger. "Where you've got people, you've got trouble."

Officer Krueger has had a hard night. Now he has parked briefly by the roadside for a smoke. He gazes down the quiet suburban street. The houses are dark and still. Everybody is asleep. The scene is utterly peaceful. A gentle wind rustles in the trees overhead.

"People," he says. "Slums or suburbs, poor or rich, it doesn't make much difference. There's only one way you're ever going to make this town crime-free. Move out all the people."

This summarized the article. Officer Krueger had said in a nutshell what the article had tried to show. But by putting the summary in quote form, by painting a little scene around the man so the reader could see and hear him talking, I engineered it so that it didn't have that dry, stale summary sound.

Within the body of an article you'll most often find yourself using quotes to support generalizations. Suppose an editor asks you to write a story on, let's say, money problems in marriage. It should be obvious to you by now that much of the article will be devoted to anecdotes, specific case histories of married couples who had some kind of trouble over money. But in between the case histories will be sections of more general material, and here's where quotes will come in handy. (Handy? No, almost essential.) In order to find the case histories, you will have interviewed psychologists, marriage counselors and other experts—including, perhaps, just plain married couples. These people will not only have told you anecdotes, but will have made interesting comments in interesting ways. These are your quotes. Use them.

You can use a quote to frame a generalization, perhaps like this: "Sometimes," says psychologist Dr. John Jones, "the problem is not too little money but too much. For instance, I recall a young couple who . . ." And, having generalized, you're launched into a case history. Or you can generalize in your own words, then follow with a quote that says, in effect, "Yes, the writer is correct." Such a structure might read:

> Sometimes the problem is not too little money but too much. "An overdose of money has hurt many marriages," says psychologist Dr. John Jones. "For instance, I recall a young couple who . . ."

Either way, the generalization is stronger and more believable than if you'd simply said it flatly in your own words and let it go at that. By hanging the generalization on a named individual, you make it sound less like a generalization. It has a sharper, more specific sound. And, as we've noted before, words from an established authority carry more weight than words from a mere writer.

Yes, you must think of yourself as "mere." The reader knows nothing about you except your name. He won't readily accept you as an authority on marriage or money or anything else. That's why there should be lots of quotes in your article.

They'll produce a cumulative effect of authority. The reader (and the editor) should come to the end of your story and think, "This writer may not have a Ph.D. in this subject, but he has certainly done his homework. By golly, he must have talked to every expert in the country! I'll bet he knows as much about it as the experts by now." And maybe you do.

Identifications

Just as with anecdotes, it is preferable to identify the people you quote—but it is allowable to use blind quotes if you don't use too many too close together. Either way, be sure to establish very firmly the credentials of the man or woman you are quoting. Tell the reader precisely why this man or woman should be considered an authority on the subject.

Sometimes this can be done in a short phrase: "Money is an important part of marriage," says economics professor Mary Smith of Ohio State University. These are credentials enough if Professor Smith is going to play only a minor role in your story. You've told why she is worth listening to on the subject of money. All right, let it go at that; the reader will accept it. But at other times, especially if the individual you are quoting is going to be quoted a lot more in the article or is going to figure in anecdotes, you may need to present his credentials more fully. In doing a *Playboy* piece on the science of sound, for example, I found on looking through my notes that a certain acoustics expert named Lewis Goodfriend had given me many of my most quotable quotes and viable anecdotes. I knew he was going to play a big part in the article, so I gave him a full introduction. I brought him onstage right after a paragraph in which I said that acoustics, for years a forgotten science, was beginning to get attention. I started to quote him, then stopped dead in the midst of his words to give his credentials:

"It's nice to be needed at last," says New Jersey sonics expert Lewis Goodfriend. He is a dark, wryly humorous man who worked on sonic weaponry during World War Two and now has his own acoustics company, Goodfriend-Ostergaard Associates. The company earns its living by such means as designing quiet offices, testing sound-deadening materials and appearing in court as an expert witness in noise-nuisance cases. It is a small outfit but—typical of the times—wealthy enough to afford a complete sound laboratory full of shiny equipment. Says Goodfriend contentedly: "In the last few years this business has gained status . . ."

Notice something else about this way of handling a quote. I've not only established Goodfriend's credentials; I've also told the reader a little about the man's looks and personality. "Dark, wryly humorous" isn't much, but it gives the reader a touch more than merely a name. As in the case where I painted a scene around a suburban policeman, this helps the reader see and hear the man talking. It makes the quote more solid, more memorable.

Scenes and sketches

Try to do a little scene-painting or personality-sketching with all your major characters' quotes. If you interview the man or woman in person, this will be easy; when you gather your material by mail or phone, it becomes more complicated but still not too hard. When I interview a man by phone and I sense he may be a major player on my article's stage, I ask him for a few personal details: age, height, weight, color of eyes. By mail, I sometimes ask for the same details, or I ask the man to send a photo of himself. Most people are flattered by this kind of request. One man became so anxious to tell me all about himself by mail that he asked his wife to send me a complete character analysis of him, as seen by her.

As for blind quotes, the same rules apply to them as to blind anecdotes. Include as much information about the person speaking as you can. And even if you can't identify him, be sure to give his credentials. "An economics professor at a major Midwestern university," or "a dark, wryly humorous sonics expert, president of a small, thriving acoustics company in New Jersey." This much identification and these credentials will usually satisfy the reader, as long as you don't ask him to believe too many blind quotes back-to-back. The reader will go along with you for a good distance, but don't ever make the mistake of thinking he's gullible. He isn't. Nor, emphatically, is an editor.

12

TRANSITIONS

I once had an argument with an architect who was designing a house for me. He won because he made an excellent point.

The house was to be a long, low, modernistic one with my office at one end and all the kids' rooms (my youngsters are noisy) clear down at the other end. For some reason that I've now forgotten, I wanted an extra chunk of house added to his original design, and he objected because the extra chunk would look like exactly that: something stuck on as an afterthought. He said, "A house is built of pieces that are put together one by one. But when it's finished, the eye shouldn't see it that way. It should look as if it grew up out of the ground whole, like a tree."

How could I argue with that? It was a universal truth. Anything man makes should look like a single thing, not a bundle of parts. Buildings, cars, novels, symphonies: the truth is applicable everywhere. And magazine articles are no exception.

It is always obvious to the writer, struggling to put his article together, that the thing he is building consists of separate pieces. But this should not be overwhelmingly obvious to the reader. The article should read as though it just *grew*.

If you have focused on your subject matter sharply and narrowly enough (see Chapter 2), you've won at least half the battle to make the story a single unit. Yet there will still be parts to be pieced together. This is why you must know how to write transitions.

Dynamic links

A transition is a group of words that dynamically links two unlike parts or carries the reader through a shift of emphasis or viewpoint. The notoriously banal phrase of Western movies, "Meanwhile, back at the ranch . . ." is a transition—in this case, between two pieces of action in two different places. The platform speaker's phrase, "Now let us turn our attention to . . ." is a transition between two chunks of subject matter. There are also many common transitions in everyday conversation:

"Say, that reminds me . . ."

"Incidentally . . ."

"Speaking of so-and-so . . ."

An article writer must be more imaginative. In the first place, good writing of any kind avoids the hackneyed, the banal. In the second place, many common transitions are static rather than dynamic. Instead of grabbing the hearer by the lapels and hurling him into the next area of subject matter, they simply stand there yawning and say, "This way, please." Take the "Incidentally . . ." locution, for example. This is so static a transition that it is almost sound asleep. It tells the reader, "Well, what I'm going to say next has only a remote connection with what has gone before. But (yawn) maybe you'll find it interesting anyway." It's very nearly a signal for the reader to stop reading.

Every article writer develops his own style of transitions. This style becomes part of his general writing style. It is his, personally. I would no more readily try to teach you my transition style than my style of dressing or combing my hair. With practice and experience, you'll develop your own transition patterns. In what follows I am going to be talking about some of my own transitions, but I don't present them as models to be copied. They are intended only as illustrations of general thoughts about transitions, and after you've read this chapter I urge you to bury yourself in a pile of magazines and see how dozens of other writers handle the same kinds of transition problems.

To talk about transitions you've got to talk about subject matter, so to save time I'm going to draw all my examples from a single article I once wrote for the Christmas issue of a major magazine. The entire issue was devoted to the subject of "Love in America," and my particular assignment was to write a story on what the editors called the "love industry"—the beauty salons, honeymoon havens, wedding caterers and other businesses that make money out of love. Because this story was built of so many diverse parts, it presented some unusually tough transition problems. It illustrates most of the common ways of approaching transitions.

The "echo" transition

In this type of transition you carry the reader across a change of subject by repeating, or echoing, a word or phrase. For example, at one point in the article I was talking about the women's figure-shaping industry—girdles and bras. I wanted to "transish" (as editors call it) from the specific to the general—from an anecdote about an individual bra designer to a paragraph of statistics on the foundation-garment industry as a whole. Here's how I did it:

> . . . The majority of women buying Marion Lukas' new bra will find it comfortable. Some won't, but they will wear it for the sake of an attractive figure.
> The Corset & Brassiere Association finds its own figures attractive too. Last year the industry sold some 230 million bras . . .

That's a weak pun. I can't resist punning, and I often use puns in echo transitions. But there's certainly no law saying you have to. The next example I'm going to show you, in talking about another type of transition, happens to involve an echo transition that isn't a pun.

The double transition

Here was a case where I was talking about women's cosmetics and wanted to "transish" to men's toiletries. I did it in two stages. In dealing with women's cosmetics I worked my way around to the subject of hair, and then I did this:

> . . . Last year, American women bought $150 million worth of hair colorings for use at home. Men bought only $10 million worth . . .

O.K. Now I've made an effortless switch from women to men. Stage One is complete. But I'm still stuck hard on the subject of hair colorings. To get from there to men's toiletries in general, I used an echo:

> . . . Men bought only $10 million worth, but manufacturers hope to goad that reluctant market to new heights in the next few years. "After all," says a Clairol lady executive, "men need love too. Right?"
>
> Right. And except where their hair color is concerned, they are admitting it at last. The men's toiletries industry finds itself in boom times . . .

The switch is now completed. I've carried the reader across a great gulf between subjects. If I'm lucky, I've done it in such a way that he hasn't been aware of taking a long journey and hasn't noticed me sweating to get him there. As a writer yourself, you know I sweated. But the reader should never know.

The Q-and-A transition

In this kind of transition, you move from one subject to another by asking a question (usually rather abruptly) and then answering it. Either in the question or in the answer, or in both, you effect your change of subject.

For instance, at one point in the love industry story I was talking about plastic surgery, and I wanted to go from a general discussion to a specific case study. I could have used the common "for example" locution, but the situation was a little more complicated than that. The case study I had in mind was supposed to show that plastic surgery is not always successful. It was the story of a girl who had had her nose pared down by a quack doctor, who had botched the job. In other words I was switching not only from the general to the specific, but from an attitude of casual observation (in which I was merely telling the reader something) to one of anger (in which I demanded an emotional response from him). I made the switch this way:

> . . . It is estimated that three times as many Americans visited cosmetics surgeons in 1965 as in 1955 to have their faces lifted, ears flattened, noses bobbed and other features changed.
> Did this win them love? It depends. In the office of a renowned plastic surgeon in San Francisco, a girl sits crying . . .

The "You-Tell-Me" transition

This is a variation of the Q-and-A—one that I personally use often because of its versatility and malleability. In this kind of transition, you ask a question but don't answer it directly. Instead, right after the question you plunge straight into the next body of subject matter. You imply to the reader that he will find the answer to the question somewhere in the material. In effect, you say to him, "*You* tell *me* the answer."

I used this style in a section of the article where I was talking about charm and beauty schools. I needed to get from here to the subject of singles bars, those places where unmarried people go to meet and be met. It was a tough transition to make, for the two subjects are far apart. Here's how I did it:

. . . A year's worth of this lovability training costs a girl about $1,000. She leaves with high hope. She has learned not only how to deport herself but how to fix her hair and how to choose the proper makeup and the right clothes.

But then what? It does little good to be an exquisite creature if there is nobody to notice. What if no man appears? What if she finds herself alone, a jewel sparkling unnoticed in the night?

The name of the place is Friday's. It is a small, dimly lit night spot in New York, tightly packed with young men and women . . .

Notice that this is a rather abrupt transition. Instead of sliding the reader into new subject matter so smoothly that he barely notices it, this transition splashes him into the new material quite suddenly and without much advance warning. Don't be afraid of doing this—occasionally. Once or twice in a story it is quite acceptable, helps relieve monotony, jars the reader awake. But don't overdo abrupt transitions. If you get into the habit of using them often (they're tempting), the result will be a jumpy, difficult style and a feeling of loose structure and general disorganization. Always remember the overriding importance of making a magazine article feel like a single thing, no matter how many or diverse its parts. Too many abrupt transitions can mar this feeling of unity.

The transitional quote

This may be the most common type of transition. It is certainly one of the easiest to use. You simply change the subject by introducing new material in the form of a quote. There is something about a set of quote marks that alerts the reader to a shift in thought. A transition that might otherwise seem too abrupt or awkward becomes acceptable when introduced with those two little upside-down commas. Quotation marks tell the reader, "This is somebody new talking—maybe about something new."

A transitional quote will often work when nothing else

seems right. At one place in my article I was on the subject of men's cosmetics, and I wanted to move from a paragraph of general information to a paragraph telling about people's reactions to the idea of men wearing scents and using hair dye. The rough draft of the piece shows how much trouble I had with this transition. I sweated over it for a whole morning. First I tried an echo transition, like this:

> . . . Colognes with swaggering names like Aphrodisia and Tiger Sweat have appeared on the market, as have male skin creams and false eyelashes. Eyebrow pencils and face colorings are under development.
> Unpenciled eyebrows have been raised over this trend . . .

I crossed that out as too strained, too corny. Next I tried a Q-and-A:

> . . . and face colorings are under development.
> Do men welcome this trend? Not all of them . . .

I didn't like that and still don't. I'm not quite sure why. (Article writing isn't as mechanical as some non-writers may believe. Sometimes you work by instinct, like a poet. If a structure of words doesn't feel right, you abandon it.) Somehow the question sounded silly at that particular place. Or maybe not silly, maybe just unnecessary, like one of those questions asked in a classroom by an overeager student trying to impress the teacher. I don't know. Anyway, out went that one. Next I tried a straight statement:

> . . . and face colorings are under development.
> Not all men are in favor of this trend . . .

Nope, that didn't do it either. It was too flat; it sounded as though I were getting bored with the subject. It sounded like the kind of transition you might find in an engineering journal or a high-school debate. Amateurish, awkward, heavy. Moreover, it was a statement of a rather obvious fact. The reader didn't need to be told the fact. What I needed to do, I finally decided, was to get the fact across in an oblique way, without actually saying it. And what better way than with a quote:

> . . . and face colorings are under development.
> "Cosmetics? Well, it looks as if they're on the way," says George Mennen, president of the Mennen Co. He appears to wince very slightly as he says it . . .

That one got me there.

These are examples of some of the more common types of transition. With practice you'll learn to fit them into your own writing style, combine them and shape them to your own purposes.

Don't let your studying end here. On your next free evening, curl up in your favorite chair with a stack of first-class magazines—not only the ones you hope to write for, but others of diverse character. Notice how different writers handle transitions, each in his own way.

And when you sit down to write your next article, handle the transitions *your* way. Build them as you might build a house, to suit your personal tastes and style. You'll probably find it difficult at first, but don't worry. All article writers find transitions difficult, and although practice can make the process a little less painful, it never becomes really easy. I have had stories bogged down for days—yes, literally days—because I couldn't find a graceful way to switch from one subject area into the next. Sometimes I've been tempted to give up entirely. "This story can't be written!" I've groaned. "It has fallen into two separate parts. There's no way to join the parts together; there's no transition in the world that can do it!" That's silly, of course. If the story was planned well in the beginning, if the basic idea of it is well focused and unified, there are bound to be transitions to hold it together. All you need to do is find them.

No, of course it isn't easy. If it were easy, millions of people would be writing articles, and editors would be buying them for ten bucks apiece. Obviously, millions of people are not writing articles. There are only a few of us. In fact, as I have said before, the shortage of good article writers is so severe that editors are offering ever higher prices to lure new literary craftsmen into the field. Good craftsmen, writers who have taken the trouble to learn the craft and are willing to work hard to turn out a good product, these people get paid handsomely. Isn't it worth the effort, even if you must sweat over a transition for three or four days?

Your answer should be "yes."

13

CHOOSING A TITLE

The title of a magazine article (editors usually call it the "head") is part of the lure and hook that catch the reader. The first thing that grabs him when he opens the printed page is the general appearance of what's called the "layout"—the artistic arrangement of illustrations, head, subhead and text blocks. You needn't worry about the layout; that's the art editor's job. If the layout attracts the reader's eye, he's likely next to glance at the illustrations and title, almost simultaneously. These tell him what the article is about, give him a fast concentrated dose of its general flavor. If the illustrations and head have done their job well, the reader's wandering eye will next drift to the lead. And if it's a good lead, he's hooked.

We have already talked about leads. Writing a good lead is *your* job, of course. Finding good illustrations is not your job, though occasionally an art editor will ask your advice or your help in tracking down possible illustrations among your research sources. How about the title? Your job or the editor's?

I'm going to answer that question by saying two things that seem flatly to contradict each other.

First, an article rarely gets printed under the writer's own title. Almost always, the magazine editors will come up with their own titles, guided by considerations such as the space available in the layout, the nature of the illustrations, and other things beyond the writer's ken.

Second, even though your title will in all likelihood be thrown away, you still have to write a good one.

Why? To grab the editor.

Catching the editor's eye

The articles editor of every big magazine that accepts free-lance material has a steady avalanche of manuscripts and outlines piled onto his desk. A few are marked for special attention and prompt action: articles from writers under contract; articles from celebrities. But the bulk of the editor's pile can be handled in any order and at any speed that suits his whim or convenience. Every once in a while during his wearying week, he'll catch up with all his immediate deadlines, and then he'll spend an afternoon going through his "anytime" pile. His object, though he seldom achieves it, is to get to the bottom of the pile and sit there for an hour and admire his beautiful clean desk top.

He goes through the pile fast. He takes an article and reads the title and lead. If he finds no music there, he may skim the rest of the story, hoping it can be made viable (oh yes, hoping hard: he *needs* good articles) but no longer in a very optimistic frame of mind. If the article doesn't seem interesting he may sit awhile and think about it, trying to estimate the amount of "in-the-shop" work that might be required to make it printable. Finally, in most cases, he'll turn the unsatisfactory manuscript over to his secretary, and she'll send it back to the writer with a rejection slip or a short, kind letter saying "No, thanks."

But suppose he comes upon an outline or an article with a lovely, crisp, high-impact title. He'll become optimistic right away. Seeing a good title, he'll immediately think two things: (1) this sounds like a writer, and (2) this sounds like a good article subject. He will read the lead with hope. Even if the article as a whole disappoints him somewhat, he may still have his original feeling of hope. He'll be reluctant to abandon something that started so well and will think long and hard about ways in which the story might be fixed up—and in the end, instead of rejecting it, he may send it back to the writer with detailed suggestions for a revision.

When I was doing some summer editing at the *Post*, I saw a dozen or more cases in which potentially good writers had hurt their chances by writing bad titles. One dog-eared manuscript sat on my desk for several weeks. It was titled "Dogs." A couple of other editors had had it on their desks for a while and had never got around to reading it because it sounded totally uninteresting. The general feeling was that nothing titled "Dogs" could possibly be worth reading. I shared the feeling when the manuscript landed on my blotter. I put off reading it. I was sure it was a washout. I was tempted to reject it without even reading past the title. But finally, one morning, my conscience got the better of me, and I picked up the story and gave it a quick skim, not with the hope of finding it printable, but simply to find some specific reason for rejecting it. And I was surprised. It was a charming little story with an odd, intriguing focus that had been nowhere apparent in the title. It dealt with certain aspects of the dog-breeding business. The writer, a woman, had a clear, sharp, wryly humorous style that any magazine would have been proud to print. Though we could not use that particular story because we had another in inventory dealing with a similar subject, we wrote to the woman and virtually begged her to try us again.

The case was unusual because the title was so bad and the story so good. It was hard to believe both had been written by the same woman. As things turned out, the bad title cost the writer nothing but several weeks' suspense while she waited for our reaction to her article. But suppose it had been only a moderately acceptable story instead of a superb one. The whole editorial office was predisposed not to like it because of its title. If it had been only moderately good, it would almost certainly have been bounced with a rejection slip. With a better title, the writer would have received less curt treatment—maybe revision instructions, maybe a check.

Three guidelines

How do you write a good title? There are three things to bear in mind. First, a good title is short and crisp—as a rule of thumb, six words or fewer. Second, it tells what the article is about, as precisely as possible within its obvious limitations. Third, it has some quality of music or surprise or impact that makes it a grabber.

The title "Dogs" obeys the first rule very nicely. But it fails to obey the second. It says only that the article is about dogs in general; it doesn't say what the focus is, what aspect of this big general subject is to be examined. As for the third rule, that title is roughly as grabby as a dead jellyfish.

The best way to write a title is, usually, to leave it until last. Sometimes an article idea will occur to you with a ready-made title, but not often. In most cases your best bet is to go ahead and write the article with no title. At some point in the writing a word or phrase will jump up at you, and that's your title.

For example, I had no title in mind—not even any vague ideas—when I sat down to write a *True* story about an oil-well firefighter. As I neared the end of the article I still had no title, and I was beginning to get a little worried. But the title suddenly hit me when I wrote the last sentence: "Even today, Kinley is known on oilfields around the world as the man who snuffed out hell." There was my title: "The Man Who Snuffed Out Hell."

This turned out to be one of those rare cases in which the article was printed under the writer's original title. Notice the points that title has in its favor. It isn't brilliant, but it obeys the rules: It's short. It says that this story (1) is focused on an individual man and (2) on a single episode in his life having to do with (3) putting out a fire. And it says so in an imaginative way. It wouldn't have been a good title if it had read, "The Man Who Extinguished A Large Oil-Well Fire." There's no music in that.

"Grabitude"

There are many ways of giving a title that quality of music, or what one editor friend of mine calls "grabitude." Basically, it is a process of figuring out some unusual or startling way to express a thought. If the thought itself is unusual, the title can be in plain pedestrian language. For example, the title "I Shot My Grandmother" is written in unimaginative language, but it stands up as a good title because the subject itself is so bizarre. It can grab a reader though it isn't imaginatively expressed. But with a less bizarre subject, the words themselves must do more work. For instance, an article about kite flying would not sound compellingly interesting if you called it simply "Kite Flying." When I wrote such an article for *True*, I called it "The Windhookers." That word "windhookers" is an unusual one. The reader must puzzle over it for a second or two before he can guess what the article is about. It has a more dramatic quality than "Kite Flying." The article eventually appeared in *True* with the editors' title, "The Manly Art of Windhooking."

Some writers like to jazz up their titles by using poets' techniques, such as rhyme ("Fearless Fred and His Six-Dog Sled") and alliteration ("Patsy's Pink Ping-Pong Parlor"). This is all right, though you must be careful not to let it get corny. In general, rhymed and alliterative titles are more appropriate for humorous or light articles than for serious ones.

Advance titling

What about outlines and queries? In most cases (see Chapter 4), you sell the basic idea of an article before you write it, by means of a query letter or a more formal outline. What part does a title play in this initial selling effort? The answer is simple. If you know what your title will be at the time you are writing the outline or query, by all means include it. If you don't know what the title will be, omit any mention of it—or use a tentative title.

A formal outline usually bears some kind of title. I prefer to write informal query letters, but when I do turn out an outline, I try to think up a tentative title for the article I want to sell. I head the outline with the words "Article Outline," and, just below, put the tentative title. In the case of the kite-flying article, my tentative title was "The Kite Fraternity." Not a very jazzy title, and I knew it. When I wrote the complete article, I took pains to think up a better title.

A query letter is like any other letter: it usually bears no title. Thus there's no need even to think about a title when you write such a letter. But if you happen to have a title in mind, tell the editor about it in an informal way: "Under the possible title of 'The Windhookers,' this story would probe the thoughts and feelings of kite fliers . . ."

Editors realize that most good titles are generated during the actual writing of the complete article, and they don't expect an outline or query to include a reader-grabbing title. In fact, once the editors have come to know a writer and his work, they will accept a query from him written in abbreviated, telegraphic style—a style bearing no relationship to the careful writing they'll expect in the finished article.

But a finished article *should* have a good title. Even if you have pre-sold it by outline or query, the editor has not obligated himself to buy it. He has obligated himself only to read it optimistically and to work with you on revisions if he believes your first version has shown enough promise. Thus, even though an editor has said, "Yes, we'd like to read it," you're still up against the need to make that article just as compelling as you can. It must be compelling all the way through—starting with the title.

14

RINGING DOWN THE CURTAIN: ENDINGS

There is only one law about the endings of magazine articles: they must be *satisfying*.

All through this book I've been urging you to be specific, but article endings are hard to be specific about. I'm not sure I really know what I mean by "satisfying." It's something you feel, more an emotion than something you can analyze. It's a color, a drift of atmosphere, an inner impact.

I've asked a dozen or more editors about this problem of endings—editors of *TV Guide, Esquire, True, Playboy,* and others, all first-class magazines piloted by first-class professionals. If these men don't know how to end a magazine article, nobody in the world does.

The answer I got from all these editors was, in brief, that I'd asked an embarrassing question. "I know a good ending when I read one," each man said in his own words, "and I know a bad ending when I read one. But the difference? The mechanics? The rules, the magic blueprint? There you've got me. All I know is, a good ending satisfies."

Fortunately, the feeling of satisfaction is so common to human beings that it does not need to be—if, indeed, it can be—analyzed. If an ending gives you this feeling, it has done its job. It is an ending that feels like an ending; it comes down with a nice hard final thump; it completes the unit that the article started out to be.

To help you understand this virtually indefinable feeling, I can prescribe an evening's exercise for you. Gather a bundle of good magazines and a couple of newspapers. Read a magazine article, then a news story, then another article, then another news item—and so on until you're immersed in the two kinds of writing. You'll notice a major difference in the endings. Every good magazine article will end with a solid bang. But newspaper stories don't end; they only stop.

Newspapers and magazines

I was a newspaperman myself once, and I do not mean to downgrade newspapers by making this comparison. I only want to point out that these are two different kinds of writing, done in different ways for different purposes. A newspaperman is trained to write his story with all its elements arranged in order of decreasing importance, so that it can be cut off at almost any point as space limitations dictate. But when an editor is cutting a magazine article for space reasons, he normally cuts down the middle but leaves the lead and the end alone. He does not want to touch the ending, because he knows it is necessary for the reader's satisfaction. Without it, the article simply will not have that feeling of unity, or the esthetically pleasing *wholeness* that a good article must have.

As I did in the chapter on transitions, I am going to give you some examples of common ending types taken from my own articles. But, as with transitions, don't think of my endings as models to be copied. I present them here only to help you start thinking about the problems and possibilities of finales. By understanding *how* I constructed certain endings and *why* and with *what* materials, and then by reading other writers' endings to see what *they* did, you'll begin to develop a basis for building finales of your own. Yours should not sound like mine or like any other writer's. Yours should sound like yours.

Types and styles and techniques

The summarizing quote is probably the most common way of ending a magazine article. You simply scramble through your memory or your notebook until you find some quoted words that seem to express the theme of your article in a nutshell. This quote becomes your ending.

Toward the end of my article on the love industry, I found myself describing some scenes of life in a honeymoon hotel. I had visited this hotel and stayed there three days. (I had also taken my wife with me—a fascinating experience, since we'd been married for fourteen years at the time.) The two owners of the hotel were friendly and talkative men, and they were also interesting characters—one small and quiet, the other big and hearty. Each had said several things to my wife and me that could conceivably have been made into an end quote. I finally decided on two quotes that not only summarized the article neatly but also, as a bonus, gave the reader a small revealing glimpse of the two partners' personalities and relationship. Here's how the finale went:

> . . . They, too, are on a honeymoon of sorts. Their business marriage seems to have achieved a state of perpetual bliss. "We're the only good Jewish-Irish partnership in the Poconos!" shouts O'Brien, fondly dropping a large hand on his partner's shoulder. Morris Wilkins grins shyly. Love has made them millionaires.
>
> "It's a wonderful business," says Wilkins.
>
> "It's great!" shouts O'Brien. "The love business! Great!"

The quote-and-booster is another common ending. You use it when, as often happens, you can't come up with a quote that quite does the job by itself. You can usually find half a dozen quotes that almost do it, but none that can stand alone. So you pick one of them and add a few words of your own to give it that extra oomph. In my *Playboy* story on sound and noise, for example, I started the ending by quoting an acoustics expert who had bulked large in the story, and then switched to my own words, like this:

"There's a lot still to be done in this business," Lewis Goodfriend told a reporter recently as they strolled down a sidewalk on the way to lunch. "There are two main avenues of research: learning how to use sound, and learning how to get away from it when it isn't wanted. Actually, I think we're just on the threshold of—"

But it was twelve o'clock, and a noon whistle began to screech from a building nearby, and the rest of Goodfriend's words were lost in the din.

The anecdotal ending is highly satisfying—provided you have a good anecdote with which to construct it. If, during the course of research, you pick up an anecdote that neatly summarizes or illuminates your theme, save it for the end. In a *True* article that I wrote in collaboration with a Washington newsman, John Barron, we used as our ending an anecdote that seemed to illuminate our subject starkly. The article was about an international munitions merchant named Sam Cummings, a tough-minded man who sells guns and other arms throughout the world despite interference from many governments and private antagonists. The article told of his early struggles, his love of guns, his toughness, his final success and huge wealth. It ended like this:

. . . and never in his life has he been known to abandon a major purpose. When he wants something, he gets it.

Back in his early days, when he was in London, Cummings used to stop and look longingly in the window of Churchill's, Ltd., an august old gun firm. Displayed in that window were two rare, ancient flintlock pistols that any gun collector would have mortgaged his soul to own. One day young Sam walked in and asked the price. Churchill's coughed politely, barely managing to hide the amused smile that curled its lip, and told him the guns had no price.

In succeeding years, as fortune began to smile on him, Cummings returned to Churchill's whenever he was in London. Each time he offered a higher price. Each time he was coolly rebuffed.

Two years ago he decided he'd fooled around long enough. He bought Churchill's.

The split-anecdote ending is harder to pull off and much less common, since it isn't easy to find anecdotes that lend themselves to the technique. But when you can engineer such an ending, it wraps up the article as tidily as a Christmas package. What you do is to start telling an anecdote in the early pages of your article, maybe even in the lead. Halfway through the anecdote, you stop. You run the rest of the article, and finally you return to the anecdote and complete it in the last paragraphs.

Obviously, to do this, you need a type of anecdote that breaks naturally into two parts. The first part must have its own strong structure, so that it can stand by itself. Finishing this part, the reader must believe that the anecdote has ended. As he finishes the article, the second part sneaks up and takes him by surprise.

I used such an anecdote in a *True* story about mental institutions. *True* is a magazine that slants all its stories strongly toward the male viewpoint, and the theme of the article was that most states' laws make it possible for a jealous or embittered wife to get even with her husband by having him declared insane and railroaded into a mental institution. Early in the article, just after the lead, I told the story of a man named Fred W., whose wife believed he was being unfaithful to her. Though Fred was as sane as you and I, she contrived to have him locked up in a mental ward.

The reader could now consider the anecdote ended. I had simply treated it like an illustrative anecdote, a specific example of the legal wrongs that the article was about. It stood by itself, this first part of the Fred W. story, and the reader could read on and forget it. But toward the end of the article, in a section where I was talking about attempts to reform the laws, I suddenly brought poor old Fred onstage again:

> . . . But legal reforms move slowly. In the meantime, let every man watch out for himself.
>
> Fred W. and Gilbert B. [another character in another anecdote] failed to be careful enough in advance, and as a result were trapped before they knew what was happening. But Fred, at least, learned his lesson.
>
> Fred was eventually released from the lockup. He got a new job. He knew his wife could have him re-committed at will; so, on the quiet, he got in touch with a lawyer . . .

And the second part of the anecdote went on to tell how Fred contrived to turn the tables on his wife, with the help of the misogynistic lawyer and a friendly psychiatrist. The last paragraph:

> It ended where the lawyer, perhaps, had foreseen it would end. At a hearing in the early summer of 1960, Fred's wife was adjudged insane and shipped off to an institution.

In effect, the whole article was enclosed inside this one split anecdote. The article was wrapped up, a cohesive unity.

The prose-poetry or "purple" ending, just like the purple lead (see Chapter 9), is hard to bring off successfully. You use it most often in the kind of article in which your main purpose is to elicit some emotional response from readers rather than give them information or spur them to action. Such a piece was one I wrote for *True* on the subject of kite flying. The main intent of the article was to plumb the souls of kite fliers, find out what drew them to this obscure, ignored sport. I started it off with an anecdote about the dean of American kitesmen, a New York advertising executive named Will Yolen.

Toward the end I started talking about Yolen again, and then I said:

> Most of all, though, Will Yolen loves to fly kites. In this he is a true windhooker, and you'll find his likes all over the world—though you'll have to look hard, for their numbers are pitifully small. The windhooker is a lonely man, delighted to find another of his persuasion as close as a hundred miles away. His neck has a permanent kink from looking upward. His face is sunburned. He has a faraway look in his eye. Give him a 10¢ kite and a ball of twine, lead him to a lonesome field with open skies above, and you won't see him again until it's time for the evening drink. And maybe, if the winds are steady, you won't even see him then.

Some writers are good at writing purple endings and write them often. I don't consider myself particularly good at it. I attempt such endings but rarely—only when nothing else seems to do the job. In this business, you have to know your own limitations and be strongly aware of your own tastes. If you like prose-poetry and feel comfortable writing it, by all means try a purple ending once in a while. But avoid such endings if they feel awkward to you. Hardly anything has a more amateurish sound than a badly written patch of purple.

Like actors but to a lesser degree, all writers have a touch of show-off in them. That's one of the things that makes us writers. We all want the world to listen to us, pay attention to us, admire our singing phrases. That's all right, but we must keep ourselves under tight rein. It's a great temptation to spatter an article with purple patches and to have a great big gaudy splash of purple at the end. But magazine editors are not chumps. They know writers, and they know that writers like to show off. When an editor comes across a purple patch, his immediate inclination is to reach for his blue pencil and start amputating. Almost by definition, a patch of prose-poetry adds no hard new material to the article—no new facts, no new specifics. As one editor grumped at me once, "Damn it,

Gunther, if my readers want to read poetry, they buy a poetry book. They don't buy this magazine!"

So rein yourself back hard when you start to write a purple ending. Keep it very, very short. If you write it long, you are only wasting words. Most of them will end in the editor's wastebasket.

The echo ending is built of the same kinds of materials as the echo transition. You pick some word or phrase that has been repeated often and prominently in the article, and you weave it into the final sentence in some meaningful or surprising way.

I did this, for example, in an article I wrote not long ago on trade names—how companies pick names for their products, by what reasoning processes, with what results. The key word in this whole story was "name." Toward the end, I talked about companies' efforts to protect their trade names from "going generic"—becoming ordinary lower-case words in public usage, as has happened to one-time trade names such as aspirin and escalator. I mentioned a dictionary, published in the early 1960's, which spelled many trade names such as Kleenex and Jeep without their capital initials, and then I quoted an official of the Brand Names Foundation who complained bitterly about this:

> "It's hard work these days to find a good name for a product," he said, morosely. "People should be more careful about spelling trade names with the proper upper-case initials. When I saw all those names lower-cased in that dictionary, I felt—I felt—" But the emotion was so intense that he couldn't put a name to it.

Notice that this is a variation of the quote-and-booster ending. In this particular case, the booster is the echo.

You can construct an echo ending in a more formal way than that. You can deliberately design the article in such a way that it almost mechanically leads to a pre-planned echo ending. In a *True* article on the subject of gold, for example, I knew what the last paragraph was going to be before I even wrote the lead. The last paragraph was going to be a single word: Gold. So I carefully and deliberately salted the article with other occurrences of this same one-word paragraph. I'd tell an anecdote, and right after it I'd start a new paragraph and say, "Gold!" I used the one-word paragraph to help effect transitions from one section of the story to the next. And finally, I closed like this:

. . . It's the bloodstained metal. The metal that can make you rich. Or dead.
Gold.

The straight statement ending is one that you should handle with care. It's easy to write: no hunting for quotes or anecdotes, no delicate structuring of echoes. This type of ending is simply a few sentences in your own words. Easy—but dangerous, for it is the type most likely to fail.

It fails most often because the writer tries to make it into a summary of the article: "And now we've learned all about gold. We've learned that it was first used in coins 2,000 years ago, that much blood has been shed over it, that . . ." This summary style of ending a magazine article became obsolete several decades ago—and good riddance to it, too. It's flat, boring, useless. *Never* attempt to write a last-paragraph summary in your own words.

Another problem with the straight statement ending is that it tends to get long-winded. You're tempted to philosophize in it, or to use it for tying up loose ends—like one of those dreadful last chapters in bad murder mysteries, where the detective tells how he solved the crime, and the book drones on for pages beyond what should have been the end. With a summarizing quote, on the other hand, you can't drone on, for the quote cannot be expanded. With an anecdotal ending, you are less likely to inflict boredom on the reader, since the anecdote will carry him along with its own momentum. But a straight statement ending can become a gummy mass of words—no ending at all.

If a straight statement seems right for your article—if it seems like the best way to express some final thought—observe three simple rules: (1) Make up your mind that this ending can express only one thought, and decide what thought it is to be. (2) Write it just as briefly as you can. (3) A day or two later, take a pencil to it and make it still briefer: cut it to the bare bone.

Does it satisfy?

Lying on my desk right now is the rough draft of an article I wrote for *True* about a man named Myron Kinley, who specializes in putting out oil-well fires. The article focuses on a single fire that Kinley battled years ago in Europe. It is essentially a nonfiction adventure narrative, and in this kind of story a straight statement ending often seems right. It can be simply a statement of the last piece of action in the chronology, much like the endings of old-time Western novels: ". . . and Cactus Schmaltz rode off into the sunset." You'd think such a statement would be easy to write without your getting long-winded, but it isn't. My first attempt at this ending shows me desperately trying to tie up a lot of loose ends in one big bundle:

Myron Kinley's hands and face were badly blistered. He had himself salved and bandaged by a doctor, spent a few days resting, finally said goodbye to Lupa and Chupp and all the other men who had fought the fire at his side. With his $50,000 fee in his pocket, he headed back to Tulsa and the comforts of home. Newspapers had already reported his victory over the enormous blaze, and his name was becoming a familiar one wherever oilmen gathered. His reputation had been made—and it shows no signs of fading even today.

They still talk about him under the derricks. Kinley is known on oilfields all over America—indeed, all over the world—as the man who snuffed out hell itself.

If you want to learn how to write bad endings, that's a good one to copy. It rambles, it drones, it says all kinds of unnecessary things. Who cares whom Kinley said goodbye to? If his hands and face were blistered, obviously he sought medical attention, so why bother the reader with this silly little fact? If the fire had been as big as the article says, obviously newspapers would have reported it and obviously this was one means by which his reputation was established. Isn't the reader bright enough to figure this out for himself?

When I read this ending two days after I'd written it, I realized how bad, how unsatisfying, it was. I cut out most of the nonsense with a pencil, and this is how it eventually appeared in print:

Kinley went home to Tulsa with blisters on his face and $50,000 in his pocket. He also took with him a reputation that still shows no signs of fading. Even today, Kinley is known on oilfields around the world as the man who snuffed out hell.

That still isn't what I'd call a swinging finale. Its main virtue is that it is short. It gets its thought across and stops. In its way, it satisfies.

15

WRITING STYLE

Of all the things I have tried to say in this book about article writing, style is probably the least teachable. The very act of teaching it tends to kill it, for style is personality. My style is my personality transferred to paper; your style is yours. If you tried to develop your style by mechanically copying other writers' literary tricks and mannerisms, you would probably turn out a dead mass of words. What you must do is sit down at your typewriter and simply write until what you have written feels like you. Write and write and write. Try this, try that. Experiment—wildly, if the mood seizes you. Finally, you'll evolve a style that feels comfortable, that works, that feels big enough and strong enough to tackle any subject in the world. When you have that, it's your style.

Personality on paper

Recently, at a meeting of the Society of Magazine Writers, an editor of a major women's magazine said that he'd like to see more articles written by novelists, playwrights, poets. What he was saying was that magazine writers as a group tend to copy each other's style, perhaps unconsciously, and that as a result, too many articles sound like too many other articles. He said he was afraid that magazines might grow monotonous if this trend were not halted. He appealed for fresh, even frankly experimental, new styles.

I have heard other magazine editors say the same thing often in the past few years, and you can read the results in most big magazines today. More than at any other time in the two decades I've been in this business, there is room in magazines for stylistic innovators. And this is yet another reason why you should evolve your own style in your own way.

Three essential characteristics

I'm not going to try teaching you style, but there are a few general hints I can give you. There are some characteristics that all good magazine article styles have in common, and chief among these are *clarity, force* and *flavor*.

Clarity is nothing more than the quality of being easily understood. Every sentence of an article should have this first characteristic. The other two elements, force and flavor, cannot be injected into every sentence but should be embodied in the article as a whole. Force is the technique of saying something hard and loud, grabbing the reader by the lapels and shouting it at him. Flavor is the essence of the writer's personality, the element that makes words chewable instead of flat, mealy, mushy.

The sentence, "Everybody was sad," has clarity but no force or flavor. The sentence, "Cry bitter, trees, all tears!" (from a poem by a teen-age girl) has force and perhaps some flavor but not much clarity. Gertrude Stein's famous phrase, "Pigeons on the grass, alas!" has a great deal of chewable flavor but little force and no clarity—at least, not the directly understandable kind of clarity that a magazine article requires.

Each writer must approach the problems of clarity, force and flavor in his own way, with his own (ideally) inimitable style. Just as an example, let me show you how I approached a certain style problem. I was writing a *Playboy* article on computers, and I was telling a story about a computer that broke down. Halfway through the anecdote, my writing style broke down, too. The article went like this:

"Oh my God!" croaked a network TV director in New York. He seemed to be strangling in his turtleneck shirt. Here he was, on the air with the desperately important election night coverage. Competing with the two enemy networks to see whose fearfully fast, magnificently transistorized electronic computer could predict the election results soonest and best. Live coverage: tense-voiced sweating announcers, papers flapping around, aura of unbearable suspense. And then, suddenly, the computer broke down.

The director and his aides were panic-stricken . . .

There is a beautiful example of mushy writing. The anecdote seemed to me to start out with sufficient clarity, force and flavor. It kept up its momentum until it got to ". . . aura of unbearable suspense." And then it seemed to wind down like a tired clock. The sentence that begins "And then, suddenly . . ." is clear enough, and so is the sentence that begins the next paragraph. But clarity is all you can concede to them. They're flat and uninteresting.

"See here, Gunther," I told myself, "there's got to be a better way to say it." So I tried this:

. . . aura of unbearable suspense. While the whole country watched what appeared on the TV screen, trouble suddenly broke loose behind the screen. The computer broke down.

The director and his aides nearly broke down too . . .

Nope. That business about screens—on them, behind them—lacked clarity. The flavor I'd been striving for didn't come across, and the whole structure was still totally lacking in force.

I stared long and hard at that disappointing echo transition —the "broke down" business. Something was wrong with it, and I thought maybe I could fix the whole structure if only I could engineer that transition better. I tried half a dozen other versions. Finally I hit upon a different echo, and after tinkering with it for a while I came up with something that satisfied me:

. . . aura of unbearable suspense. Whole country watching. And what happens? The damned computer quits.

Oh my God. The computer rooms disintegrated in panic . . .

This is my style of writing. It shouldn't be yours, and I don't present it here with the hope that you'll admire it or copy it. All I want to do is show you what is meant by style and what it involves for you, the writer. To achieve a good style you have to be eternally dissatisfied with your own work. Avoid saying things in the easiest way. Constantly ask yourself if there is not a better way—clearer, more forceful, more flavorful.

If you want to have some fun with style and some good, profitable exercise, too, take a flat, simple statement such as "George went down the street with Alice." Without adding more than a few words to it, try to give it force and flavor without diminishing its clarity. When you hit upon a version that satisfies you, what you've done is to say it in your style. Your way of saying it would doubtless be quite different from mine—and for that reason an article by you and one by me, printed in the same magazine, would sound different (or should, if we've done our jobs well).

I don't want to say much more about clarity, force and flavor because almost everything I say will inevitably have reference to my own style. Rather than listen to me, you should think about these elements and play with them in your own typewriter. Meanwhile, here are some specific hints that may help you achieve the style you want.

Avoid monotony

Variety is important in sentence length, word length and sentence structure. About fifteen years ago a number of journalism textbooks appeared on the market all at once, urging people to use short sentences and short words almost exclusively. One book even went so far as to suggest a word-counting formula by which a writer could tell whether he was writing well. If his sentences averaged so many words or fewer, he was a good writer; if he overshot the limit, he was not. This all seemed pretty silly to me. Length is only one factor that affects the clarity of a word or a sentence. The word "representative" is a long word—five syllables—but it isn't hard to read, pronounce or understand. Similarly, the first sentence of Lincoln's famed Gettysburg Address is quite long, but it is perfectly clear. What makes a sentence clear is its structure—the orderly, careful way in which its elements are hung together.

Instead of trying to make all your words three or fewer syllables long and all your sentences eight words or fewer, strive for variety. After a few short sentences, use a long one; in the midst of some long words, a short one. And try for variety in other ways. To avoid the monotony of sentences that all run subject-predicate-object, turn some of them inside out and upside down. (*Time* Magazine is famous for its own style of doing this: "Up from his chair rose old Joe Smith. . . .") Break up the drone of words now and then by stopping short with a question mark. Instead of writing, "If you want to live longer, medical men and scientists insist you should stop smoking," try "Stop smoking? Yes, if you want to live longer." Your own style will dictate the best methods for you to use to avoid monotony.

Don't be afraid of colloquial language

You aren't writing a legal document or a company president's speech; you're writing a magazine article. As long as you don't overdo it (which would create its own irritating monotony), you can use slang occasionally. You can use mild cusswords now and then in some magazines, as I did in my *Playboy* computer anecdote. You can use incomplete sentences: "Stop smoking? Yes, if you want to live longer." You can even coin your own words. Here's an example from my New York *Times*

Magazine article on a commuter railroad in trouble: "It is bankrupt and rapidly getting rupter."

Again, your personal style will tell you how much and what kinds of colloquialisms you use. Some writers use many; their styles are loose, easy, slangy. Other writers use very few; their particular styles are more coolly controlled, more studiously correct. Either way, if the writer handles his style well, he fits colloquial words and phrases into it so that they sound perfectly right. If a slangy or unofficial word doesn't feel comfortable to you, the chances are it won't sound comfortable to the reader, because it somehow doesn't belong. In such a case, find another word.

Avoid clichés

This is essentially a specific case of what I said before about striving for flavor—avoid the easy locutions that come to mind first. A cliché is something so easy to say that thousands of people have said it over and over again until we're all sick of it. It's a faded old clump of soggy words like "scarce as hens' teeth" or "hot as Hades" or "hook, line and sinker." Sometimes we use clichés without even thinking about them. I do so myself, much as I hate them. The only sure cure is to go through the rough draft of your article and mark the clichés with a big black pencil. Then find a better way to say it—*your* way.

A cliché need not be a set group of words; it can be also a pattern of words, phrases, or expressions. For example, there's the murder-mystery cliché: "He was (adverb) dead." It may read "He was quite dead" or "He was very dead" or, worse yet, "He was very, very dead." I keep promising to throw the offending book or magazine out the window if I come upon this dreadful locution again, though so far I've restrained myself. Then there's the woman-describing cliché: "Miss Jones, an (adjective) (hair type) of (age) . . ." It may read "Miss Jones, an attractive blonde of 36 . . ." Surely, there are other important characteristics of women than these. With a little extra work, a little thinking about flavor, a writer should be able to lift himself out of this easy-rolling rut.

Avoid mannerisms of punctuation

One irritating mannerism that gives an article an amateurish appearance is the overuse of quote marks. A writer will use quotes to emphasize a word or phrase, and sometimes even to emphasize a cliché. One sentence that I recall from a beginner's article submitted to *The Saturday Evening Post* went like this: "After 'sleeping like a log' all night, he got up refreshed and 'plunged' back to work." Quotes used in this way only annoy readers.

Too liberal a use of italics or underlining has the same bad effect. Here's another amateur's sentence: "But in a *nuclear war*, only a few people could *hope* to survive." It's all right to use italics once or twice in an article for special emphasis, but when you use them too often they lose their punch entirely. In a well-built sentence, the rhythm of the words themselves will supply all the emphasis you need. Italics are a refuge of neophyte writers who don't trust their own ability to build sentences well—and when an editor sees an article sprinkled with italics or underlines, he knows it's the work of an amateur.

A similar lack of self-confidence leads beginning writers to use other kinds of punctuational noisemaking devices such as exclamation marks and rows of dots. The simple sentence, "He was dead" is written in flat language, but it has force because of its arresting subject matter. It can't be made more forceful by changing it to "He was . . . dead" or "He was dead!" Any time you feel the urge to make noise with punctuation in this way, ask yourself whether you can achieve a better effect simply by arranging the words well. As an exercise, read a dozen or so articles in major magazines and see how many exclamation marks you can find. You'll see that the professionals use exclamation marks very rarely, except to emphasize certain kinds of quoted material ("Stop!" he yelled). Seldom will you find a professional writer emphasizing his own words this way. He is confident that his words carry their own built-in emphasis and need no extra help.

Confidence underlies every good style. The only way you can achieve confidence, as any good teacher will tell you, is to practice.

16

THE MECHANICS OF THE TRADE

There's an old aphorism to the effect that "clothes don't make the man." Almost everybody acknowledges that this is probably so. The same *you* exists whether you're neatly dressed or sloppily dressed. Your mind, your internal character remains the same whether you're in evening dress or raggedy dungarees. Yet, like most aphorisms, this one is too much of a generality to be taken entirely seriously. Clothes don't change you, but they certainly change other people's impressions of you. When you're applying for a job you don't turn up in old sneakers and with an unwashed face.

Paper proxy

Magazine articles should be properly dressed too, for the same reasons. When you submit an article to an editor in the hope he'll buy it, that article is you on paper, applying for a job. This paper proxy of yours must be neat and attractive, must have a professional look. It must tell the editor favorable things about you before he starts to read it. If it does not tell him these favorable things he'll read it negatively.

These are the little mechanical details that, if ignored, could hurt your chances of selling:

Typing: Use a ribbon that types in solid black, not gray. A new ribbon costs only a dollar or so. Buy one as soon as your old ribbon begins to fade. Editors read prodigious amounts of typed material, and at the end of a long day their eyes hurt. They are not favorably disposed toward a dim gray manuscript.

Double-space any manuscript that is to be more than two pages long. (Letters and queries can be single-spaced.) On the first page of your article manuscript, start with the title and your name about one-third of the way down the page. This leaves a field of white space at the top for editorial jotting. (Don't worry: editors won't scribble on it if they're going to reject it. But if they buy it, they will want room for notations, printer's labels and the like.)

The first page of your manuscript should be an attractive, neat job of typing with no errors, erasures or crossings-out. This is another reason for starting a third of the way down the page: you have less first-page typing to do. On succeeding pages, a few crossings-out per page are quite all right. It's preferable to cross out and retype a mistyped word than to try erasing it. When you erase a word and type over the erasure, the result can be hard to decipher. But if you simply type X's through the word and start all over again, there will be no question about which spelling you intend.

Paper: Use a standard grade of white paper. Don't use a flimsy, crinkly-surfaced or onionskin paper. And don't use those new "erasable" papers. These are fine for some uses in which you want clean erasures, but they make no sense for manuscripts. In the first place, there's never a need to erase on a manuscript. More important, erasable papers smudge too easily, and the ink can be smeared by other things besides an eraser—a thumb, for instance. After an erasable-paper manuscript has been handed around an editorial office for a few days, it looks like something salvaged from a flood.

Stacking: Number the pages consecutively, putting the numbers anywhere but the upper left-hand corner (in case there's a paperclip there). Don't staple the pages together; use only a paperclip. In reading your article, the editor usually likes to unclip it and turn the pages over flat on his desk.

Mailing: Don't fold the pages. Mail them flat with a cardboard stiffener. (Queries and outlines can be mailed folded, like ordinary letters.) Send all manuscripts by first-class mail. There are other, cheaper classes of mail, but they aren't cheaper by enough of a margin to make up for their disadvantages. First-class mail travels fast and is handled with care. Cheaper classes of mail may lie about in bags and boxes for days before delivery—and, during the process of waiting and getting shifted around, may get trampled, crumpled and torn. One of the little irritations of editors' lives is that of trying to read wrinkled manuscripts that won't lie flat on a desk. So spend the few extra nickels for the red-carpet mail service. After all, it costs very little to mail a 20-page manuscript first-class. When you consider what price that manuscript might bring, isn't it worth the small extra cost?

Waiting: Having launched your article upon the U.S. Mail, try to forget it. Work on another article. Go to movies. Build a bookcase. Whatever you do, be patient. It's most unlikely that you'll get any editorial response within the first two weeks, and the average waiting time is about four weeks. This is the time it takes, in most editorial offices, for any potentially acceptable article to be passed around to the various men and women who must read it. (Totally and obviously unacceptable work gets shipped back to the writer much faster.) If you find yourself getting fretful and impatient, console yourself with the thought that your work is being read with care, and that care takes time.

In some magazine offices, each potentially acceptable story gets a "comment sheet" paperclipped to it, and as the article makes its rounds of the office, each editor writes down what he thinks of it and whether it should be bought or rejected or sent back for a rewrite. This process can take six weeks. In other offices the process is less formal. Editor A reads your article and wanders into Editor B's cubicle with it and says, "Take a look at this. I think maybe . . ." And then Editor B reads it and hands it to C with a comment, and maybe after a while C ambles down the hall to talk it over with A. This, too, can take six weeks.

Whatever you do, don't harry the editors with hey-where's-my-manuscript letters or phone calls. Bear in mind that these men and women are eagerly hunting for publishable work. If an article shows even the faintest kind of beginner's promise, they will pore over it and discuss it and do their damnedest to figure out some way of making it work. You'll only irritate them if you betray impatience.

If you've heard nothing after six weeks, then it's all right to send the magazine a quiet, friendly note asking for news. Not an angry demand, not a howl of indignation. Just a gentle jog: "I wonder if you've reached any decision yet about my article?" Usually this will get you a quick reply—even if it's only a note from an editor asking for more time.

Revisions: If your article is almost but not quite acceptable, you'll get it back with a letter saying what the editors think should be done to it. Accept this letter and its recommendations gratefully, not grumpily. Don't try to argue with the editors. In all my years in this business, I've never seen a case in which a writer changed an editor's mind about a proposed revision. Simply revise the article as the editors suggest and send the new version back to them. Along with it, send a letter thanking the editors for taking the time to help you make the manuscript acceptable. You'll be displaying a professional attitude, for which the editors will admire you. The professional feels that a good article is the product of close collaboration between writer and editor—not a solo performance by a virtuoso who is too good to need advice.

Rejections: It happens to everybody, no matter how long he has been in the trade: an article comes back with a curt "No, thanks." Take it in stride. All right, so you're blue for a day. But you'll feel better tomorrow, and then there are two things you should do:

(1) Send the editors a friendly letter, saying you're sorry this particular article didn't grab them but you've got other ideas that you'd like to try out on them soon. Let them know that you intend to keep trying, that you aren't just a one-shot amateur whom they will never hear of again. If they can look into the future and see you as a steadily productive professional in a few years' time, they'll work hard with you while you're a beginner. And (2) send the article to another magazine. Don't try to explain why you're submitting it without having queried first. Most articles are preceded by a query or outline, but a certain number come into every editorial office each week with no advance warning—"over the transom," as editors put it. Obviously these unheralded articles stand less chance of being bought than those following a query letter or submitted on an editor's invitation, but surprising numbers do find their way into print.

The law: There are three main areas of law that you should be aware of as an article writer. They are *plagiarism* or *copyright infringement* (stealing someone else's work); *libel* (the act of publishing slander); and *invasion of privacy* (exposing someone to unwanted or harmful publicity). You need not be a lawyer to stay out of these areas of potential trouble. All you need to remember, really, are two rules: play fair and play safe.

Don't use anyone else's published words without giving him full credit, and don't quote more than a sentence or two without first asking permission. Write to either the author or the publisher, explain what you are doing and why you want to quote from his text, and ask permission to do so. Enclose a self-addressed envelope or post card for the copyright owner's reply. When you get the reply, carefully file it.

As we mentioned earlier, a magazine article should not contain too many quotes from published material, and most of these should deal with what people have *said,* not what they have written or published.

Don't write anything slanderous about any identified individual or organization. As a beginning writer, you would be wise not to identify any person or institution about which you are revealing uncomplimentary facts. Use the technique of blind quotes and anecdotes instead—"A doctor in San Francisco. . . ." or "An electronics company in the midwest. . . ." Furthermore, don't quote a malicious remark made by one man about another. Merely putting the remark in quotes does not remove your responsibility for it. And be cautious about quoting unpleasant statements from newspapers. Sad to say, newspapers are generally unreliable as final sources of data. A newspaper is useful only in steering you toward stories and sources of information; you should not consider it a source in itself. Never use potentially libelous material unless you are absolutely sure you are on safe ground. *When in doubt, don't.*

And finally, in the area of invasion of privacy, don't tell a story about an identified individual unless you are perfectly sure it is all right with him. As a magazine writer, you're in the business of talking about people in the public press. You must be sure they are willing to be talked about. There is a class of people called "public figures"—movie stars, politicians, performers and entertainers, and the like—and the law holds that they have voluntarily given away their privacy. Since such a figure does not have his privacy, you obviously can't invade it. As long as you don't libel public figures, you may write about them without their permission.

But suppose you are writing about the home life of your next-door neighbor. He is a private, not public, individual. Unless you tell him beforehand that you are writing about him and unless he consents, don't.

So play fair and play safe. Write nothing about any named or identified individual unless you have personally talked to him or written to him, told him what you're writing and secured at least his tacit consent to be included. (If he answers your questions after you've told him you're writing an article on such-and-such for X Magazine, that's "tacit consent.")

Whenever you are in doubt about any of these "rules" as they apply to an article you have written, check with an editor.

Checks: And finally, when the mailman brings you what you've been hoping for, a check, accept it with thanks. Write to the editor immediately and say you hope to do a lot more work for him in the future. Even if the check is disappointingly small, don't argue about it. You won't get anywhere; you'll only make the editor angry at you so that he'll buy no more articles from you in the future. You can argue about money when you're soundly established in the article-writing business and when an editor knows that, if you don't write for him, you can write for somebody else. As a beginner, you need to make friends with many, many editors.

Payment rates

Most magazines have scales of pay that allow little flexibility or bargaining room, except at the highest levels. Obviously, if a major political figure were to offer to write an article about his thoughts on war and peace, any big magazine would pay him virtually anything he asked. In fact, if he were smart or had a smart agent, he'd be able to get magazines bidding against each other for his article. But for you and me, plain free-lance writers, the pay rates are fairly well set. A beginner gets so much, an established professional so much, a long-time contributor so much. Magazines try to pay generously—each according to its means—for they are anxious to attract writers. Whatever the size of any check you may receive, the chances are it is fair pay as that magazine sees it.

Bear in mind, too, that the turnover among magazine editors is fairly rapid. Today, an editor of the *Nowhere Gazette* may buy a story from you for $25. Thank him. Tomorrow he may phone you and say, "I've moved to the *Affluent Monthly,* and one of my jobs is to bring in new writers, and I was wondering if you . . ."

Now it's your move

I think I've said just about enough. There is a limit to what you can learn from me, even if I were the best teacher in the world. Once you've grasped the fundamentals, the only way for you to become a skilled writer of articles is to write them. So now it's your move.

Write hard. Don't be discouraged if you fail to sell your first few efforts. I didn't sell my first few, and I don't know of any article writer who did. And don't be discouraged if your first sales are to minor, low-paying markets. My first sale brought a price of $25—and since it was a collaborative effort between me and another reporter, my share was $12.50. This represented about two weeks of work. I thought, "There must be an easier way to make a buck." For a while I was disgusted by the whole idea of selling words. But once you get printer's ink inside you, it's there forever. I came back and tried again. My second sale was for $750, and that changed my whole philosophy. Now a family of five lives on what I earn as an article writer, and I can't imagine earning my living in any other way.

Don't lose your momentum once you've started. Keep your queries circulating. React to the faintest nibble from an editor. Even if he's not too encouraging, even if he says he'd like to read your finished article but can't guarantee to buy it and in fact doubts that he will, go ahead and write it anyway. The practice will do you good. And if that editor doesn't buy it, send it over the transom to other magazines. Seize any excuse to write anything. Think of yourself as an article writer and behave like one everywhere you go. Listen for ideas. Read newspapers. Ask people questions. Be nosy.

If you find it hard to write, try shifting your schedule

around. Some people write more fluently at night, others in the early morning, others at midday. With me, it's early morning. My schedule is not in step with the rest of the world. When I'm up against a deadline I go to bed right after supper and get up at 2 a.m. or even earlier. Test yourself and find when the words come easiest. You'll probably find six hours of sleep a night is plenty, and for weeks at a stretch it is possible to live on four. As an article writer, you'll find life too fascinating to waste in sleep.

Keep learning, keep improving. Read every article in every magazine you can lay your hands on. When editors turn down your work, read their letters with care. These won't be detailed letters in most cases, but sometimes they will contain some brief explanation of why the article didn't appeal. Whatever the editor didn't like, try to remedy it in your next effort. And be ruthless in editing your own work. This is very hard to do, but not impossible. You have to pretend somebody else wrote this article, and then you have to read it with sour pessimism and tell yourself what's wrong with it. There is always something wrong, no matter how long you've been in the business. Always. Even if it means rewriting the whole article—which it often does—you must admit the faults to yourself and do away with them.

Sure, it's hard work. Maybe that's why there is such a shortage of good article writers. Maybe a lot of people have toyed with the idea of writing articles and have looked at the work required and have gone away, never to be heard from again. What they didn't look at carefully enough, perhaps, was the fun and the money.

PART FOUR

Case Histories

17

ANATOMY OF THREE ARTICLES

Now I'm going to let you look over my shoulder and watch me working on three different magazine articles. This may help you see how various aspects of the article-writing craft hang together and finally produce a publishable story.

A. Article for *Travel & Leisure*

This article illustrates, among other things, an important point about the article writer's eternal search for ideas. As we saw in an earlier chapter, the search consists of two main elements: reading everything you can get your hands on and talking to everybody in sight. That second element is probably the more important. It is just barely conceivable that you might become a successful nonfiction writer without hungrily reading newspapers and magazines, but I absolutely cannot imagine how you could do it without going out and talking to other men and women. They are your richest source of ideas.

You never know what seemingly unlikely person, what seemingly banal conversation will suddenly generate a salable idea in your head. Thus you should talk to everybody: your neighbors, their kids, people who sit next to you on buses, the cop on the corner, the folks at the town hall, the checkout lady at the supermarket. As an article writer, you should go about the world with a friendly smile on your face and an attitude that says, "Tell me about yourself, your work, your thoughts."

Among the many people you should get to know are the

executives and other personnel of business concerns in your vicinity. In particular, if any nearby company is big enough to employ a publicity or public relations director, go out of your way to make friends with that man or woman. This person's job is, of course, to get the company favorably mentioned in the press. But if you take the trouble to talk and listen, you are likely to find that he or she knows much about the company's industry as a whole—about social problems affecting the industry, its relationship to various national and international events, and so on. Buried somewhere in the publicity director's head could be more than one fine story idea for you.

Late in 1974 I stopped in to have a cup of coffee with a publicity man representing Johnson Wax. My feelings were fairly pessimistic. I asked myself, "How on earth could an interesting story come out of floor wax?" What I did not know, and would not have found out unless I had gone out of my way to listen, was that Johnson is also a major producer of insect killers and repellents. As the publicity man started to talk about some work being done at the company's laboratory, I heard that voice in my head shouting, *"Story!"*

I sent a brief query letter to *Travel & Leisure*, the American Express magazine. I suggested that it might be fun to publish a story on biting bugs some time in the summer, when people are getting bitten. To publish in the early summer, a monthly magazine must receive a manuscript by (usually) March at the latest. In my query I was careful to outline my proposed schedule, pointing out that I could easily finish the article by February. The editors told me to go ahead.

The research was easy, and also fun. I began by going to my local drugstore and reading companies' names off bottles and tubes of insect repellent, to find out who besides Johnson was in the business. Some labels gave addresses. Others gave only the name of a city. In the latter cases, I found the street addresses by consulting a phone book collection in a library. I wrote each company an information-please letter.

When the replies came in (along with enough free samples to

last my family for years), I followed up with phone calls. It turned out that some companies had working relationships with biologists and other specialists at various universities. To give my article a sound of good scientific research, I wrote to these specialists for further information and talked to some by phone.

Finally I was ready to write. I had much more material than could be packed into one short article. I had a big stack of letters, advertising brochures, papers photocopied from scientific journals, and other material. I had a notebook crammed with my own scribblings. And I had a problem: how to organize all this and focus it into a magazine article.

I prowled around for a couple of days, doing nothing in particular, letting the material shift and settle and mix itself in my mind. The ending jumped up at me before anything else did. After that, the rest of the structure gradually became clear to me. I saw that I could tell my story effectively by dividing it into six main sections. I did not give titles to the sections (as I have done below), for my thinking was not that formal and exact. I knew only what the general drive and drift of each section would be, what kinds of material it would contain. And finally, on a bitterly cold January day, I rolled some yellow paper into my typewriter and began to write my summer story.

Here it is, exactly as it appeared in the July 1975 issue of *Travel & Leisure*.

MAN VERSUS INSECT

By Max Gunther

Early one spring morning, in a small Florida hotel, two men came down to breakfast in eye-catching attire. They wore women's stockings, pulled up over their pants and tightly secured around their calves with adhesive tape. The waitress who served them tried hard to be polite and studiously kept her eyes off their legs. A third man, conventionally dressed, joined them just as they were finishing their meal. As the waitress watched them leave, she couldn't contain

SECTION I: ESTABLISHMENT OF THEME

Anecdote lead also establishes the tone of voice: light, cheerful. With some subjects, it is a mistake to write too solemnly.

herself any longer. She plucked the third man by the sleeve and whispered, "Do you, um, know them?"

"You can see why we choose out-of-the-way places to stay," says Eugene Mace, recalling the episode with an embarrassed grin. Mace was one of the men so fetchingly clad in stockings. He is chief entomologist at Johnson Wax, which makes, among other things, insect repellents. On that morning in Florida, he and his colleague were on their way to a nearby swamp, where they planned to test the effectiveness of a newly compounded chemical in keeping mosquitoes off their ankles.

A roundabout way of introducing an authority.

Johnson is one of many companies, government agencies and university groups in the bug-bite business. They are all looking for ways to protect us from the hordes of carnivorous insects that puncture, slash and nibble us when we are trying to enjoy ourselves outdoors. Now that summer is here and the blood-loving hordes are on the wing, you may find this report on those efforts encouraging.

This paragraph tells the reader precisely what the article will be about—and why he should care.

The perfect, foolproof, all-bug repellent hasn't yet been invented, but it is nice to know the quest is being pursued with dedication and courage. At Johnson's laboratory in Racine, Wisconsin, where Mace and his team raise some 14,000 mosquitoes and 10,000 biting flies a day, I once watched a young assistant put his bare arm through a draw-string opening into a cage containing what looked to me like several million mosquitoes. I was later told there were only a thousand or so, but that was quite enough. With a scientific detachment that thrilled me (and also made me itch), he coolly counted "lands" and "bites" on a marked-off skin area over a given number of minutes. Then he repeated the process with the other arm, which was treated with an experimental chemical. The mosquitoes appeared to lap up the chemical with relish. The young man sighed, withdrew his arm and made some entries in a notebook.

First sentence of this paragraph is a transition into . . .

. . . another anecdote.

Reporter's "I" tells the reader I was there, doing my homework. A useful stylistic trick—but it will annoy reader if used too much.

"Doesn't it itch?" I asked.

"Sure," he said cheerfully, and then he shrugged. "Some jobs give you sore feet, some give you an aching back. Here you get itchy arms. No job is perfect."

The same passionate dedication to truth drives entomologists out into wood, field and bog, wherever they can arrange to get scientifically bitten. When offering themselves to mosquitoes they generally sit still, for the mosquito is a slow flier and fairly lazy. Other man-eaters such as the deerfly, however, seem to be drawn to moving targets. "In case you want to know," says Dr. Walter Gojmerac, entomology professor at the University of Wisconsin, "the best way to attract deerflies is to race around flapping your arms." They are also drawn to anything shiny and black, he says. For this reason, entomologists interested in the particular insect will sometimes go out and dance in meadows and forests, waving sheets of black plastic. They get questioned a lot by suspicious farmers, police and park rangers. It is a profession full of embarrassments. Still, the brave work goes on.

To get a clearer idea of the benefits this work may bring to humankind, let's look briefly at the enemy. Among insects with an appetite for human and animal blood, the most familiar nuisances are these:

The mosquito. There are several hundred species, of which about seventy live in North America. Many are vegetarian. In the carnivorous species, it is usually only the female who sucks blood. The male contents himself with plant juices or, like the common housefly, feeds on dead meat. "The female needs a blood meal to lay eggs," says Dr. Gojmerac. "Blood is her source of essential protein. She can lay a few eggs without blood, but with it she can lay a few hundred."

As almost every picnicker and backyard barbecuer knows, the female mosquito is equipped with a long, thin proboscis something like a hollow needle. With this effective instrument she can drill through one or more layers of thin summer clothing, through the skin beneath and into the blood-bearing tissues. "The proboscis is so fine that you wouldn't feel it at all," says Dr. Gojmerac, "except for the saliva that she injects into you. The saliva contains an enzyme that keeps your blood from coagulating—in effect, 'thins' it so she can drink it. This enzyme is what

Marginal notes:

Reiterating the theme.

Another authority. Article is light in tone, but I am striving to give it some solid scientific weight.

SECTION II: A "LESSON" ON INSECTS

Italic type is indicated on a manuscript by underlining. Used this way, it helps you organize complex material.

Notice the technique of shifting from my own words . . .

. . . into a quote . . . .

raises a bump and makes you itch." Some people are more allergic to the enzyme than are others, which explains why some can spend a summer evening outdoors with little discomfort while others get driven to a frenzy of itching and go to bed covered with angry-looking red bumps and patches.

The deerfly, and similar species like the horsefly and greenhead. These are large, powerful, fast-flying insects. They don't have the mosquito's type of blood-sucking equipment. Instead, this kind of fly has sharp, knife-like mouthparts called stylets. The stylets are used to slash the victim's skin—often a very painful bite—and the fly then laps up the blood that oozes from the wound.

The stable fly, also called the dog fly and beach fly. This blood-seeker is smaller than the deerfly but bites in much the same way and almost as painfully. It seems to like watery regions and is found around freshwater lakes and on ocean beaches when the wind is blowing off-shore. For reasons that aren't understood, it considers the human ankle a particular delicacy.

The no-see-um, a name given to many species of very small blood-eaters. You may know them by names such as the sand fly, the punky, the gnat, the nit. Some of these tiny species are equipped with razor-sharp stylets; others, with mosquito-style needles. Many can get through standard mosquito mesh and are greatly attracted to anybody reading by a screened window or on a porch at night.

These and other carnivorous insects have plagued humanity throughout history, and since the very earliest times, people have sought ways to escape. Historians at Union Carbide, another major maker of repellents, have combed through folklore to see what mankind did about bugs in the past. Their report is a catalogue of desperation and nearly perfect failure.

The heavy eye makeup that was popular in Cleopatra's time, say Carbide's historians, came partly from the belief that black-rimmed eyes would scare biters away or would at least keep them off the face. Field tests of the technique reveal that, in fact, its only effect is to make the

. . . and back to my own words. This relieves monotony in heavy material.

Italic type again. Notice how it acts as a transition from one block of material to the next.

A contraction: "aren't." Colloquial language is attractive, but don't let it become slangy.

SECTION III: A QUICK WALK THROUGH HISTORY

Note the transition.

Another authority—this time a large corporation.

face look odd to other humans. A somewhat later idea was the wide-brimmed, fringed hat. The movement of the fringe was supposed to frighten insects away. This didn't work either. Nor did the idea of hanging cotton balls around the house. This approach originated in the southern United States, where people thought they noticed that there were seldom many mosquitoes or flies around a cotton field. The inference was that cotton repels bugs. Unfortunately, it doesn't.

Odor was the basis of some other techniques. Until fairly recently in this century, many home-owners thought it helped to keep pans of decayed fish around their yards. The theory was that the average bug, in ecstasy over the strong fish smell, would ignore passing humans. Actual effect: smelly yards. Another approach was to eat strong-smelling foods such as garlic, thus supposedly making oneself unpalatable to any fastidious mosquito. Effect: smelly breath.

Other odor-based ideas may have been some-what more effective. Ancient Egyptians thought they noticed that certain oils and perfumes kept them from being bitten, and it may be that they stumbled on effective repellents by accident. They may have used an oil related to citronella, for instance. This oil, made from a tropical grass, demonstrably repels mosquitoes to some extent and was widely used in America until stronger repellents were developed during World War II.

However, it may also be that the Egyptians were fooling themselves. Laboratory and field tests seem to show that certain sweet-smelling perfumes, including some suntan preparations and men's shave lotions, actually attract flying insects quite strongly—or, at best, tend to nullify the effects of repellents. In any case, whether or not those old-time bug remedies worked, they often made the user more uncomfortable than if he had just gone out and let the biters bite. Some tar-based preparations burned the skin—or, ironically, produced an itching rash that felt something like the results of a massive mosquito attack. Other remedies were simply greasy and sticky. An old edition of the *Encyclopedia Americana* counsels the mosquito-tormented reader to

Transition.

A long sentence. . .

. . . followed by a short, incomplete one.

And then the same rhythm is repeated. Such linguistic games help keep the writing lively.

smear himself with citronella, oil of cedar, spirits of camphor and Vaseline. This pungent glop may have warded off not only bugs but also humans, dogs, alligators and perhaps all other earthly creatures.

> A bad sentence: trying too hard to be funny. Never stop editing yourself.

All through this long search for relief, one baffling fact has been noted again and again: some people just naturally seem to get bitten less than others. Some ancient historians reported that Cleopatra was bite-free all her life, and the same phenomenon puzzles modern Americans at beaches and picnic grounds. One man or woman may be tormented by flies, while somebody else a few feet away seems to be left blissfully alone. Why? Do some people have a skin odor or taste that repels insects?

> SECTION IV: WHAT TO-DAY'S SCIENCE KNOWS

> Article began with this aspect of the subject, veered off it, and now returns for a longer look.

> A way of introducing a subject: Ask a question . . .

To date, there are no reliable answers to the question. What does appear true is that many or most tales of bite-free people are probably exaggerated. People blessed with natural repellency may get bitten less than others, but they do get bitten. In a classic study about ten years ago, Dr. Howard Maibach and a research team at the University of California School of Medicine advertised for people who claimed they were seldom or never bitten by mosquitoes. Laboratory tests revealed that mosquitoes found these people as delicious as anybody else. Dr. Maibach and his colleagues concluded that there probably is no bite-free person in reality, only in folklore.

> . . . and then answer it.

> Note that I'm still working hard to project a sound of solid research.

But it does seem that biters, when they have a choice, will often pick one person and ignore another. It may be that a lucky man or woman with mild natural repellency will be left alone as long as he or she is always careful to go outdoors with other, tastier people. This may be the origin of the "never-bitten" myth. In another study at the University of California, guinea pigs and humans were exposed to mosquitoes simultaneously and then, a few days later, separately. When the mosquitoes had a choice, they chose humans three-to-one over guinea pigs. When there was no choice, the hapless guinea pigs got drilled just as often as the humans. The obvious moral of the story is that, if you're a guinea pig, you should never go outdoors without people.

> I originally wrote "less repellent" but changed it to "tastier" on self-editing. Never be satisfied with your first choice of words.

The same research team that performed the guinea pig study, headed by Dr. A. A. Khan, tested 100 people recruited at random and found that six were relatively unattractive to mosquitoes. However, when the same six were tested again a few weeks later, only three seemed to have kept their natural repellency. "Perhaps," suggests Eugene Mace, "your attractiveness to insects on any given day depends partly on what you've been eating." This possibility prompted a search for an "oral repellent"—a pill or drink that would make you bite-free for a few hours or days. So far, no effective oral repellent has been invented, for nobody knows what body chemicals (if any) attract or repel.

The cardinal rule: be specific. I could have said all this in general terms, but by using Dr. Khan's study, I can make it livelier.

Diet may or may not have something to do with certain other unexplained oddities. Men, on the average, seem slightly more attractive to most common American biters than do women. Young adults get bitten a little more often than the very old or very young. Baby girls are evidently less tasty than anyone else.

Other research findings are more useful because you can do something about them. But by far the surest way to ward off blood-eaters is to spread a modern repellent chemical on your skin and on areas of clothing where there aren't enough layers to protect you, such as the socks.

SECTION V: A REPORT ON MODERN REPELLENTS

Not one of my best transitions, but it gets me where I want to be.

Nearly all the best-known commercial repellents on the market today are, in one way or another, descendants of various chemicals developed by the U.S. government for use by military forces in World War II and the Korean War. One of the key chemicals is a compound generally referred to by its nickname, Deet. If you must know the full name, it is N. N. diethylmetatoluamide. Deet has a powerful and demonstrable repellent effect on many flying insects. including the mosquito. In its natural state, its odor is only mildly offensive to the human nose, and another big advantage is that it doesn't irritate most people's skin.

To enliven dull material, make fun of it ("if you must know . . .") But use this trick sparingly.

Johnson's and Carbide's well-known repellents, trade named respectively Off and 6-12, contain a lot of Deet. Both companies have recently introduced stronger repellents—respectively Deep

Woods Off and Sportsmate II—that contain still more Deet, plus other, newly developed chemicals. Another strong, second-generation repellent is made by Cutter Laboratories of Berkeley, California.

All commercial repellents contain an odor mask or perfume, plus an inert base—a cream, oil or aerosol propellant. (Though all must pass government tests and be certified safe for human use, you should be aware that most can damage varnished surfaces and certain plastics, like those often found in sunglasses.)

Parenthetical sentences often result from lazy writing. Use them very, very sparingly.

Exactly how do these repellents work? Oddly, nobody knows. "There are a lot of theories," says Dr. Gojmerac. "A logical-sounding inference would be that insects don't 'like the smell,' unquote, but there is no evidence at all that this is what really goes on. As somebody once said, 'to know what goes on in a fly's head, you've got to be a fly.' All we can do is observe the fact empirically: certain insects avoid certain chemicals."

Question-and-answer transition.

An application of repellent will usually last between two and eight hours, depending partly on how hungry the flies are and partly on what you are doing. If you move around a lot, you will rub the repellent off some parts of your body. "Because of this rubbing effect," says often-bitten Mace, "you'll see mosquitoes going first for places like the cracks between your fingers and the fold of skin in front of the elbow." Swimming and heavy perspiration will wash the protection off.

Notice the use of a quote to reinforce my own statement.

You can check on how well a given application is lasting by watching what would-be biters do in your vicinity. Professional biter-watchers say there are four quite distinct stages as a repellent slowly wears off. Stage One: a hungry bug approaches, flies around you for a while and then gloomily departs. Two: he lands on you, then flies off immediately. Three: he lands, probes or "sniffs" briefly, then goes without biting. Four: he bites. Once the first bug has bitten, others follow fairly fast, for now the repellent effect is gone.

"Gloomily departs" was originally "goes away." Keep hunting for more interesting ways to say a thing.

There are other kinds of insect-chasing products on the market besides those you put on your skin.

A weak transition. It could have been better.

Several companies make killer sprays for bushes and porch screens, and you can also buy products that burn and give off a bug-repellent smoke. These can give you a cocoon of protection in a confined area such as your backyard. But they may be less useful on breezy days or in open, treeless areas such as a beach, and of course they can't help unless you plan to stay within an established cocoon. The spread-on-the-skin type of repellent lets you take your cocoon with you.

If a few bugs bite you despite all the chemical help you have bought, there is still one last thing you can do. There is a technique that was undoubtedly developed long before the ancient Egyptians began experimenting with oils and eye shadow, and it is effective against all biters. You slap them.

SECTION VI: ENDING

I knew what this ending would be before I even wrote the lead. It obeys the rule: it satisfies.

B. Article for *Playboy*

It is often very hard to look back and try to recall where an article idea originated. This one had been floating about in the back of my head for years: an article saying that electronic computers are not really as good as all the propaganda would have us believe. I'd been avoiding the idea because I knew that, unlike the *True* piece on men's toiletries, it would not be easy to research: I would not have companies lined up at my door, begging me to mention their products in the article. Quite the opposite, in fact. Unless I was extremely careful, computer manufacturers would refuse to say a word to me. So for years I had kept this potentially good idea locked up where nobody could see it and where it couldn't cause me any trouble.

Market-watching

I think I might have sold it to any of several magazines. But in this case, when I finally unlocked it, I tried it on *Playboy*. This happened because, as every article writer should,

I conscientiously study all my likely markets with great care. I buy every issue of every magazine that I write for or hope to write for, and I read the issue from front cover to back-page ad. If you do this studiously, you will see subtle shifts of emphasis from month to month; and if your eye is sharp, you may see such a shift developing before other article writers see it. Then you can jump in with an article on a subject that no other writer would have considered a good bet for that magazine.

Playboy is a stellar example of the need for this kind of market-watching. It is a very young magazine. It has found a brilliantly successful basic formula for itself and is already one of the wealthiest and most successful (and highest-paying) magazines in the world. Yet, being young, it is still searching, still experimenting with its own personality. It has undergone several perceptible changes in the past five years. Not everybody has noticed these changes—and, in fact, even many article writers haven't. A general impression seems to be that *Playboy* devotes itself almost exclusively to sex, liquor and sport cars. The magazine is inundated with queries and fiction in these general subject areas, and it is quite obvious that most of these writers simply haven't been reading the magazine carefully enough. I promised myself more than a decade ago that I'd never make this mistake.

It was some time in early 1966, I think, that I began noticing a shift in *Playboy*. The magazine was becoming more interested in current science. It had published science-fiction of high quality for years, but it had not carried many science articles. Now it was beginning to do so—and I jumped in with queries. I began to sell to *Playboy* regularly: all articles on science. One suggestion I made to the editors was my "computers-aren't-so-hot" idea, and it turned out that the editors had been thinking of such an article themselves. "We'd like to run two articles on computers side by side," one editor told me. "One will be yours, saying that computers have been overrated. The other will take the opposite viewpoint: that computers are superbrains."

It made me a little nervous to know there would be another article in the same issue, arguing with mine. But I couldn't quarrel with the editors' proposal. Here was a perfect example of skillful editing. The editors had taken a good idea and, by adding a second idea to it, made it twice as good.

I began my research, as always, with the *Readers' Guide*. About six or seven years before, there had been a minor flurry of articles on my subject. In these I found the names of a few sources: professors in universities, management consultants and others who appeared willing to say uncomplimentary things about computers. I wrote and phoned these people and got some usable material, but not much. I went to New York, bought a cup of coffee in a luncheonette, and by this inexpensive means rented one of the luncheonette's phone booths as my office for the day. In the phone book yellow pages, I hunted down names of others who might have something to tell me about computers. (There was a whole category of listings headed "Data Processing Consultants," for example.) I phoned these sources and began to get more and better material. One consultant became so intrigued with the concept of my article that he asked me to meet him for lunch. My research was producing results.

But at the end of that day I still felt dissatisfied. The major failing of what I'd done so far, I felt, was that all my sources were people on the periphery of the computer business. They were outsiders, looking in. The article, as it was now taking shape, lacked that good "inside-y" feeling, the feeling of penetration to the heart of the subject. If I tried to write the article at this point, it would have a vague, wishy-washy tone. Readers would think: "This writer hasn't done his homework. He has poked around the edge of the computer business and gathered all his information second-hand, from a safe distance. It doesn't sound as though he has ever actually *seen* a computer."

Correct. I hadn't—not on this assignment, anyway. I saw that the article could not be written successfully unless I actually went to computer manufacturers themselves: IBM, Honeywell, RCA and others. But how could I get them to talk to me? How could I ask them to reveal uncomplimentary facts about their own products?

The answer was simple, when I finally saw it.

I asked myself: What is this article really about? Will it say, "Computers are no good"? Of course not. It will say, "Computers aren't as magical as the stories have claimed." There was an important difference between the two concepts, and this difference was the horse that I rode into the heart of the computer business.

I phoned a public relations man at Honeywell. I told him in general what my article was to be about, and then I said, "Honeywell doesn't want to be known as a company that makes exaggerated claims, does it?"

"Of course it doesn't," he said. "No company does."

"So, from a public relations point of view, it would be good for Honeywell to get into the position of urging honesty. Am I right?"

"You are."

"I hoped I was. What you want to say in public, in other words, is something like this: 'See here, everybody, there have been a lot of highly imaginative articles and science-fiction stories written about computers. These are all great fun, but let's not let our imaginations run away with us. Let's not expect more of computers than they can really do. Let's praise them for what they *can* do, but let's not call them superbrains or any nonsense like that.' "

The public relations man chuckled. "That has been our party line for years," he said. "You want to come up here and visit us?"

And so it went at IBM and other companies. By approaching

them this way, I got all the material I needed. Much more than I needed, in fact.

Here is the article I wrote, as it appeared in the October 1967 issue of *Playboy*:

COMPUTERS: THEIR BUILT-IN LIMITATIONS

By MAX GUNTHER

"Oh, my God!" croaked a network-TV director in New York. He seemed to be strangling in his turtleneck shirt. It was the evening of Election Day, 1966, and the director's world was caving in. Here he was, on the air with the desperately important Election Night coverage, competing with the two enemy networks to see whose magnificently transistorized, fearfully fast electronic computer could predict the poll results soonest and best. Live coverage: tense-voiced, sweating announcers, papers flapping around, aura of unbearable suspense. The whole country watching. And what happens? The damned computer quits.

Oh, my God. The computer rooms disintegrated in panic. Engineers leaped with trembling screwdrivers at the machine's intestines. The director stared fish-eyed at a mathematician. A key-punch girl yattered terrified questions at a programmer. Young Madison Avenue types rushed in and out, uttering shrill cries. And the computer just sat there.

The story of this ghastly evening has circulated quietly in the computer business ever since. You hear it in out-of-the-way bars and dim corners of cocktail parties, told in hoarse, quavering tones. It has never reached the public at large, for two reasons. One reason is obvious: Those concerned have sat on it. The second reason is less obvious and much more interesting.

When the initial panic subsided, the director freed some of his jammed synapses and lurched into action. He rounded up mathematicians, programmers, political experts, research girls and others. And he rounded up some hand-operated

I. ESTABLISHMENT OF THEME

Anecdotal lead uses loose, slangy language to convince reader this won't be a dry scientific treatise. It takes effort to hook reader into this kind of story.

Cusswords are useful for emphasis—in the proper stylistic situation. Use sparingly.

"Yatter" is a coined word: another useful stylistic trick in the proper place. But be sure the meaning isn't ambiguous.

adding machines. "All right," he said, "we'll simplify the calculations and do the whole thing by hand. This may be my last night on TV; but, by God, I'll go on the air with *something!*"

And so they perspired through the long, jangling night. The network's election predictions appeared on the screen just like its competitors'. The director and his aides gulped coffee, clutched burning stomachs and smoked appalling numbers of cigarettes. They kept waiting for an ax to fall. Somebody was bound to notice something wrong sooner or later, they thought. The hand-cranked predictions couldn't conceivably be as good as the computerized punditry of the competition. Maybe the hand-cranked answers would be totally wrong! Maybe the network would become the laughingstock of the nation! Maybe. . . . Oh, my God!

Well. As history now tells us, the entire poll-predicting razzmatazz was the laughingstock of the nation that November. None of the three networks was wronger than the other two. When the half-gutted director and his fellow conspirators skulked out of bed the next morning and focused smoldering eyes on their newspapers, they at last recognized the obscure little facts that had saved their professional lives:

An electronic computer, no matter how big or how expensive or how gorgeously bejeweled with flashing lights or how thoroughly crammed with unpronounceable components, is no smarter than the men who use it. Its answers can never be better than the data and formulas that are programmed into it. It has no magical insights of its own. Given inadequate data and inexact formulas, it will produce the same wrong answers as a man with an aching head and an adding machine. It will produce them in a more scientific-looking manner, that's all.

Over the past ten years, it has been fashionable to call these great buzzing, clattering machines "brains." Science-fiction writers and Japanese moviemakers have had a lovely time with the idea. Superintelligent machines take over the world! Squish people with deadly squish rays! Hypnotize nubile girls with horrible mind rays,

Note use of italics and exclamation mark in quote. They are rarely useful otherwise.

Odd stylistic situation: a quote that is neither direct nor indirect. Playing with language like this avoids monotony.

"Razzmatazz": another unofficial word.

Note that this is a blind anecdote. Yet the reader is told it refers to one of the three networks. This is enough identification to make it credible.

The article stops, draws a deep breath and expresses its theme in one long sentence . . .

. . . followed by short ones.

Abrupt transition out of lead: restatement of theme.

Still using a slangy tone and direct-indirect quotes.

baby! It's all nonsense, of course. A computer is a machine like any other machine. It produces numbers on order. That's all it can do.

Yet computers have been crowned with a halo of exaggerated glamour, and the TV election-predicting circus is a classic example. The Columbia Broadcasting System got into this peculiar business back in 1952, using a Remington Rand Univac. The Univac did well. In 1956, for instance, with 1/27 of the popular vote in at 9:15 P.M., it predicted that Dwight Eisenhower would win with 56 percent of the votes. His actual share turned out to be 57.4 percent, and everybody said, "My, my, what a clever machine!" The Univac certainly was a nicely wrought piece of engineering, one of the two or three fastest and most reliable then existing. But the credit for insight belonged to the political experts and mathematicians who told the Univac what to do. It was they, not the machine, who estimated that if Swampwater County went Democratic by X percent, the odds were Y over Z that the rest of the state would go Democratic by X-plus-N percent. The Univac only did the routine arithmetic.

Which escaped attention. By the 1960s, the U. S. public had the idea that some kind of arcane, unknowable, hyperhuman magic was soldered into computers—that a computerized answer was categorically better than a hand-cranked answer. As the TV networks and hundreds of other businesses realized, computers could be used to impress people. A poll prediction looked much more accurate on computer print-out paper than in human handwriting. But, as became clear at least to a few in 1966, it's the input that counts. Honeywell programing expert Malcolm Smith says: "You feed guesswork into a computer, you get beautiful neat guesswork back out. The machine contains no Automatic Guess Rectifier, or Factualizing Whatchamacallit."

The fact is, computers are monumentally dense—"so literal," says Smith, "so inflexible, so flat-footed dumb that it sometimes makes you want to burst into tears." Smith knows, for he

II. PROVING COMPUTERS ARE OVERSOLD
Returning to subject of lead anecdote for another kind of thematic restatement. This material could have been put into the lead anecdote itself—but then the lead would have been too long.

I originally wrote "super-human." Then I hunted for a less overworked word and came up with a coinage.

Still pounding theme into reader's head. He must *not* lose sight of it.

Statements by the article writer . . .

. . . are supported by an authority.

spends his life trying to make the great dimwits cogitate. To most people, however, computers are metallic magic, wonderful, tireless, emotionless, infallible brains that will finally solve mankind's every problem. Electronic data processing (EDP) is the great fad of the 1960s and perhaps the costliest fad in history. Companies big and small, universities, Government agencies are tumbling over one another in a gigantic scramble for the benefits of EDP. They believe EDP represents, at last, instant solutions to problems they've wrestled with for decades: problems of information flow, bookkeeping, inventory control. And they're hounded by dreams of status. To have a computer is "in." Even if you're a scruffy little company that nobody ever heard of, you must have a computer. Businessmen meeting at conventions like to drop phrases such as "My EDP manager told me" and "Our programing boys think," and watch the crestfallen looks of uncomputerized listeners.

General evidence of first part of theme: that computers are considered magical.

It's a great business to be in. Computer makers shipped some 8000 machines in 1965 and 13,700 (3.75 billion dollars' worth) in 1966. There are over 30,000 computers at work in the country today and there will be (depending on whose guess you listen to) as many as 100,000 by 1975. It's a boom business in which young salesmen can buy Cadillacs and Porsches, while their college classmates in other professions are still eating canned beans in one-and-a-half-room flats. The salesmen don't need any unusual qualifications to strike it rich: just a two- or three-year apprenticeship, a sincere hard handshake, a radiating awareness of belonging to an elite group and a good memory for a polysyllabic vocabulary. (You don't sell machines; you sell "systems" or "systems concepts," or "integrated functional solid-state logic systems concepts." They seem to cost more that way.)

Statistical evidence.

The salesmen are all business. They sell machines on a severely pragmatic level, maybe exaggerating their products' worth sometimes but, in general, avoiding any unbusinesslike talk about "superbrains." Computer manufacturers as a whole, in fact, avoid such talk. To their credit,

III. PROVING COMPUTERS AREN'T "BRAINS" Slow transition starts with salesmen . . .

they have struggled from the beginning to keep things in perspective, have publicly winced when imaginative journalists compared computers with that odd gray mushy stuff inside the human skull. "Don't call them brains! Please, *please* don't call them brains!" shouted IBM scientist Dr. Arthur Samuel at a reporter once. "But listen," said the reporter, "don't they——" "No, they don't!" howled Samuel. "Whatever you're going to say they do, they don't!" (Samuel, now at Stanford University, had won unwanted fame for programing an IBM machine to play checkers.) "Computers are just extremely fast idiots," says logician-mathematician Richard Bloch, a former Honeywell vice-president now working with Philadelphia's Auerbach Corporation. Bloch, a lean, dark, ferociously energetic man who smokes cigars incessantly, first tangled with the machines in the early 1940s, when he helped run Harvard University's historic Mark 1. "On second thought, 'idiots' is the wrong word. It suggests some innate thinking capacity gone wrong. Computers have no thinking capacity at all. They're just big shiny machines. When will people learn that machines don't think?"

Maybe never, though men like Bloch never tire of saying so. "A computer can multiply umpteen umpteen-digit numbers a second," says Bloch, "but this is only blind manipulation of numbers, not thinking. To think about a problem, you've got to understand it. A computer *never* understands a problem."

Arthur Samuel, for instance, tells about an early checkers-playing experiment. A British computer was given a simple set of rules in arithmetical form. Among other things, it was told that a king is worth three points, an uncrowned piece one point. It played an ordinary undistinguished game until its human opponent maneuvered a piece within one move of being crowned. Then the machine seemed to go mad.

Somewhere in its buzzing electrical innards, a chain of "reasoning" something like this took place: "Oh, my goodness! If my opponent gets his piece into the king's row, he'll gain a three-point king where he had only a one-point man

. . . ends on the subject I want to talk about.

The reporter was me. But somehow it seemed awkward to intrude myself into the article by saying "shouted . . . at me."

Bloch will be quoted often from here on, so I give his credentials at length and add some personal glimpses.

Anecdote introduced by standard "for instance" transition.

before. In effect, this means I'll lose two points. What'll I do? (*buzz, buzz* . . .) Ah! I'll sacrifice one of my uncrowned pieces. The rules say he must take my piece if I offer it, and this will force him to use his move and prevent him from getting his man crowned. I'll have lost only one point instead of two!"

So the cunning computer sacrificed a man. The human player took it. The situation was now exactly the same as it had been before, so the computer slyly sacrificed another man. And so on. Piece by piece, the unthinking machine wiped itself out.

The computer had proved itself able to manipulate some of the arithmetical and logical formulas of checkers. But it had failed in one supremely important way. It simply didn't understand the game. It didn't grasp what no human novice ever needs to be told: that the basic object of a game is to win.

The trouble with computers is that they *seem* to be thinking. While cars, lawn mowers and other machines perform easily understood physical tasks, computers seem to be working with abstract thoughts. They aren't, of course; they are only switching electric currents along preordained paths. But they produce answers to questions, and this gives them a weird brainlike quality.

People expect too much of them, as a result, and this seriously worries some scientists. The late Norbert Wiener, coiner of the term "cybernetics," was particularly worried about the increasing use of computers in military decision making. Referring to machines that can manipulate the logical patterns of a game without understanding it, he once wrote that computers could win some future nuclear war "on points . . . at the cost of every interest we have at heart." He conjured up a nightmarish vision of a giant computer printing out "WAR WON: ASSIGNMENT COMPLETED . . ." and then shutting itself down, never to be used again, because there were no men left on earth to use it.

Secretary of Defense Robert S. McNamara has hinted at similar worries in the years-long argument about our famous (but so far nonexist-

Partial restatement of theme also serves as the first stage of a double transition.

Transition complete: I'm on the subject of war computers, which the editors specifically told me to cover.

Pace is slowing down.

ent) Nike-X missile-defense system. Neither full-fledged hawk nor dove, McNamara favors a leisurely and limited building of Nike bases. He wants the U. S. to have some defense against a possible Russian or Chinese ballistic-missile attack, but he fears that an all-out missile-building program will involve us in a ghastly game of nuclear leapfrog with the Soviets—the two sides alternately jumping ahead of each other in countermeasures and counter-countermeasures until the radioactive end. One trouble with missile and anti-missile systems, as McNamara once expressed it to a group of reporters, is that "the bigger and more complex such systems get, the more remote grows man's control of them." In a nuclear-missile war, so many things would happen so fast, so much data would have to be interpreted in so limited a time that human brains could not possibly handle the job. The only answer for both the U. S. and Russia in a missile arms race would be increasing reliance on automatic control—in other words, on computers.

Pace very slow. Sentences long; material more general than specific.

The last war might, in fact, be a war between computers. It would be a coldly efficient war, no doubt. A logical war: Score 70,000,000 deaths for my side, 60 megadeaths for your side; I'm ahead; your move, pal. How could we convey to the machines our totally illogical feelings about life and death? A country is made of people and money, and the people may properly be asked to give their lives for their country, yet a single human life is worth more than all the money in the world. Only the human brain is flexible enough to assimilate contradictions such as this without blowing a fuse.

A large modern computer can literally perform more arithmetic in an hour than can a football stadium full of human mathematicians in a lifetime, and it makes sense to enlist this lightning-fast electronic help in national defense. "But," said Norbert Wiener shortly before he died in 1964, "let us always keep human minds in the decision loop somewhere, if only at the last 'yes' or 'no.'"

This philosophizing has gone on long enough. It must end soon, or readers will quit.

The U. S. Ballistic Missile Early Warning System (BMEWS) is an example of the kind of

Material gets more specific. Sentences grow shorter. Pace picks up.

setup that worried Wiener. Its radar eyes scan sky and space. Objects spotted up there are analyzed automatically to determine whether they are or aren't enemy missiles. The calculations performed by computers—distance of the objects, direction, checkoff against known craft—take place in fractions of a second, far faster than human thought. It all works beautifully most of the time, and this has led some enthusiasts to suggest going one step further in automation. "If BMEWS can spot enemy missiles by itself," they say, "why not hook up one more wire and have BMEWS launch *our* missiles?" But U. S. military chiefs have so far agreed with Norbert Wiener. There is a subtlety in the human brain that no computer seems likely ever to duplicate.

A few years ago, an officer was monitoring a BMEWS computer station in the Arctic. It was night. The rest of the staff was in bed. Suddenly, the computer exploded into action. Lights flashed, a printer chattered, tape reels whirled. The officer gaped, horrified. The machine was signaling a massive missile attack.

Illustrative anecdote. Pace picks up more.

There are self-checking devices and "redundant" networks in the BMEWS, as in any other large computer system, and the officer had no logical reason to suspect a mechanical breakdown. There could be little doubt that the computer was actually reporting what its far-flung radar eyes saw. The officer's orders were clear: In an event like this, he must send a message that would mobilize military installations all over the United States. Global war was only minutes away.

The officer hesitated. Questioned later, he couldn't explain why. He could only say, "It didn't *feel* right." And he gambled time to wake other staff members. One of them dashed outdoors to look at the cold, clear, starlit Arctic sky, ran back indoors, examined the computer's printout, conferred with the others. Standing there in that antiseptic room full of shiny electronic equipment, the small knot of men made what may have been the most important decision in all the history of the world to date. They decided to wait.

They waited 30 awful seconds. The missile attack came no closer.

The officer's feeling had been correct. This was no missile attack. Unaccountably, through a freakish tangle of circumstances that should never have happened and could not have been predicted and was not fully unraveled until weeks later, the computer and its eyes had locked onto something quite without menace: earth's friendly companion and goddess of love, the moon, peacefully coming up over the horizon. If computers alone had handled the affair, the earth might now be a smoldering radioactive cinder. Because of a man and his slow, strange human brain and its unfathomable intuition, we are all still here.

When a computer makes a mistake, it's likely to be a big one. In a situation where a man would stop and say, "Hey, something's wrong!" the machine blindly rushes ahead because it lacks the man's general awareness of what is and isn't reasonable in that particular situation; such as the time when a New York bank computer, supposed to issue a man a dividend check for $162.40, blandly mailed him one for $1,624,000; or the time when a computer working for a publishing company shipped a Massachusetts reader six huge cartons neatly packed with several hundred copies of the same book; or the time when an IBM machine was constructing a mathematical "model" of a new Air Force bomber that would fly automatically a few dozen feet off the ground. Halfway through the figuring, it became apparent that the computer was solemnly guiding its imaginary aircraft along a course some five feet below the ground. ("Goddamn it," roared General Curtis LeMay at one of the scientists, "I asked for an airplane, not a plow!") Or the time when——

Well, everybody makes mistakes. In general, society is most worried about mistakes made by war computers in the BMEWS style, for the potential result of a mistake in this field is the end of the world. Fearful imaginings such as *Fail-Safe* have expressed this fear, and most U. S. military planners share the fear and are cautious in their approach to computers. But no such colossal danger haunts computer users in science and business; and in these two fields, the great

Short "flash-by" section gives more examples.

Transition by interruption. Subject changes from military to civilian computer uses.

dumb machines have been pushed willy-nilly into all kinds of applications—some more sensible than others. A New York management-consultant firm, McKinsey and Company, exhaustively studied computer installations in 27 big manufacturing companies four years ago and found that only nine were getting enough benefits to make the machines pay.

"Sometimes computers are used for prestige purposes, sometimes as a means of avoiding human responsibility," says computer consultant John Diebold. Diebold, at 41, is a millionaire and an internationally sought-after expert on "automation" (a term he coined in the early 1950s). "Scientists and executives have discovered that it's impressive to walk into a meeting with a ream of computer print-out under your arm. The print-out may be utter nonsense, but it looks good, looks exact, gives you that secure, infallible feeling. Later, if the decision you were supposed to make or the theory you were propounding turns out to be wrong, you simply blame the computer or the man who programed it for you."

Professor David Johnson of the University of Washington is another well-known computer consultant who worries about what he calls "the mindless machines." He is amused by the fact that his engineering students seek status by using IBM cards as bookmarks—just as, 20 years from now, they will seek it by buying IBM machines for their companies. He praises computers for their ability to manipulate and organize huge masses of data at huge speeds. But, "What the computer does," he says, "is to allow us to believe in the myth of objectivity." The computer "acts without excessive hesitation, as if it is sure, as if it knows. . . ." A man who isn't sure can often make people think he is, simply by coming up with a bundle of factual-looking print-out. He hides his own bad brainwork, says Professor Johnson, by "sprinkling it with *eau de computer.*"

Worse, Professor Johnson says, the growing availability of computers tends to make some researchers in scientific institutions avoid problems that don't lend themselves to machine han-

Statements by the writer . . .

. . . supported by an authority.

Quote transition.

Credentials of quoted authority in the middle of his quote.

Transition by indirect quote.

dling: Problems involving human values, problems of morality and aesthetics, subtle problems that can't be translated into arithmetic and punched into those neat little snip-cornered cards —all these get left out of the calculations. The tendency is to wrench reality around and hammer it into a nice square shape so the inflexible machines can swallow it. Professor Johnson glumly cites the case of a computer-headed robot recently developed by a major agricultural-research center to pick tomatoes. It clanks along briskly, picking the juicy red fruits faster than a whole gang of human workers. The only trouble .is, its blind, clumsy fingers break the tomatoes' skins. The agricultural scientists are now trying to solve the problem. By making the robot more gentle? No, by developing thicker-skinned tomatoes.

"It simply isn't accurate to call these machines 'clever,'" says Robert Cheek, a chief of the Westinghouse Tele-Computer Center near Pittsburgh. This is one of the biggest computer installations in the world, designed to handle Westinghouse's huge load of corporate clerical and accounting work, and it generates science-fictionish visions of an office of the (if the cliché may be pardoned) future. It's an entire modernistic building housing almost nothing but computing equipment. Clerks and secretaries who once populated it have been crowded out, and now it smells like the inside of a new car. Bob Cheek, a slight, mild man, looks small and lonely as he paces among the square whining monsters; and it is tempting to imagine that the machines have subjugated him as their slave. Actually, he is little more awed by this great aggregation of computing power than by an electric toaster. "Artificial intelligence?" he will say in response to the question he has heard too often. And he will look at his machines, think of the man-hours required to make them work, take off his glasses, rub his weary eyes and chuckle sourly.

Logician Richard Bloch is an example of high human intelligence. He learned chess at the age of three and is now, among other things, a Life Master bridge player and a blackjack shark. He once tried to teach a Honeywell computer to play

The anecdote is blind, but the source is identified.

Question-and-answer style ends anecdote with a satisfying thump.

Quote transition.

If you use a cliché, make sure the reader knows you know it's a cliché.

Echo transition: "intelligence."

bridge. "The experiment gave me new respect for the human brain," he recalls wryly. "The brain can act on insufficient, disorganized data. A bridge novice can start to play—badly but not stupidly—after an hour or so of mediocre instruction, in a half-drunken foursome. His brain makes generalizations on its own, reaches conclusions nobody ever told it to reach. It can absorb badly thought-out, unspecific instructions such as, 'If your hand looks pretty good, bid such and such.' What does 'pretty good' mean? The brain can feel it out. Now, you take a computer——"

Bloch pauses to chew moodily on his cigar. "A computer won't move unless you tell it every single step it must take, in excruciating detail. It took me more than a hundred pages of densely packed programing before I could even get the damned machine to make the first bid. Then I gave up."

The quote was getting long, so I broke it in half with a personal glimpse of the man.

The fact is, human thinking is so marvelous and mysterious a process that there is really not much serious hope of imitating it electronically —at least, not in this century. Nobody even knows how the brain works. Back in the late 1950s, during the first great soaring gush of enthusiasm over computers, journalists and some scientists were saying confidently that the brain works much like a very small, very complex digital computer—by means of X trillion tiny on-or-off switches. It remained only for IBM, Honeywell and Rem Rand to devise a monstrous mile-high machine with that many switches (and somehow figure out a way to supply its enormous power needs and somehow cool it so it wouldn't melt itself), and we'd have a full-fledged brain. But this was only another case of wrenching reality around to fit machinery. There is no reliable evidence that the brain works like an EDP machine. In fact, evidence is now growing that the basic components of human thought may be fantastically complicated molecules of RNA (ribonucleic acid), which seem to store and process information by means of a little-understood four-letter "code."

IV. A "LESSON" ON COMPUTERS
(You often need a "lesson" section in science articles, to give readers the necessary technical background. But keep it short and zingy.)

Referring back to previous material this way helps tie the article's parts together.

The human brain is uncanny. It programs itself. It asks itself questions and then tells itself how to answer them. It steps outside itself and looks back inside. It wonders what "thinking" is.

No computer ever wondered about anything. "It's the speed of computers that gives the false impression that they're thinking," says Reed Roberts, an automation expert who works for a New York management-consultant firm, Robert Sibson Associates. "Once a man has told a machine how to process a set of data, the machine will do the job faster than the man's brain could; so fast, in fact, that you're tempted to suspect the machine has worked out short cuts on its own. It hasn't. It has done the job in precisely the way it was told, showing no originality whatever."

For instance, you can program a machine to add the digits of each number from 1 to 10,000 and name every number whose digits add up to 9 or a multiple of 9. The machine will print out a list instantly—9, 18, 27—acting as though it has gone beyond its instructions and cleverly figured out a short cut. This is the way a man would tackle the problem. Instead of routinely adding the digits of every number from 1 to 10,000, he'd look for a formula. His brain would generalize: "Every time you multiply a number by 9, the result is a number whose digits add up to 9 or a multiple of 9. Therefore, I can do my assignment quickly just by listing the multiples of 9 and ignoring all other numbers." Is this what the computer did? No. With blinding speed but monumental stupidity, it laboriously tried every number, from 1 to 10,000, one by one.

In this example lies one of the main differences between thought and EDP. The human brain collects specific bits of data and makes generalizations out of them, organizes them into patterns. EDP works the other way around. A human programmer starts the machine out by giving it generalizations—problem-solving methods or "algorithms"—and the machine blindly applies these to specific data.

It is by no means easy to program a computer, and one of the great problems of the 1960s is a severe shortage of people who know how to do it. There are now some 150,000 professional programmers in the country, and computer owners

Echo transition: "wonder."

My statements are supported by an authority . . .

. . . who in turn is supported by an example. You can't go too far in this process of supporting the general with the specific.

First stage of a double transition. I want to get onto the subject of programing.

Transition complete.

are pitifully crying for at least 75,000 more. One estimate is that 500,000, all told, will be needed by the early 1970s.

The shortage is understandable. Computer programing is self-inflicted torture. The problem is to make a mindless machine behave rationally. Before you can tell the machine how to solve a problem, you must first figure out how your own brain solves it—every step, every detail. You watch your brain as it effortlessly snakes its way along some line of reasoning that loops back through itself, and then you try to draw a diagram showing how your brain did it, and you discover that your brain couldn't possibly have done it—yet you know it did. And there sits the computer. If you can't explain to yourself, how are you ever going to explain to *it*?

We're still in the "lesson" section, but note how I'm laboring to make it sound unlike a lesson.

I thought for half an hour about italicizing "it." It was a question of sentence rhythm that still troubles me. Maybe I should have reworked the sentence.

Aptitude tests for would-be programmers contain questions that begin, "If John is three years older than Mary would have been if she were three and a half times as old as John was when . . ." This is the kind of human thought that must precede the switching on of a computer. The machine can't add two plus two unless there are clever, patient human brains to guide it. And even then it can't: All it can do is add one and one and one and one and come up with the answer —instantaneously, of course. No computer can multiply; all it can do is add, by ones, too fast for human conception. Nor can any computer divide; it can only subtract, again by ones. Feed it problems in square roots, cube roots, prime numbers, complex mathematical computations with mile-long formulas—it can solve them all with incredible rapidity. How? Essentially, by adding or subtracting one, as required, as often as required, to come up at once with an accurate answer it might take a team of mathematicians a thousand years to obtain—and another thousand to check for accuracy. It never invents its own mathematical short cuts. If it uses short cuts, they must be invented and programed into it by human thinkers.

Question-and-answer style helps lighten heavy material.

A computer's only mental process is the ability to distinguish between is and isn't—the presence or absence of an electric current, the *this way* or *that way* of a magnetic field. In terms of human thought, this kind of distinction can be conceived as one and zero, yes and no. The machine can be made to perform binary arithmetic, which has a radix (base) of 2 instead of our familiar 10 and which is expressed with only two digits, 1 and 0. By stringing together yeses and noes in appropriate patterns, the machine can also be made to manipulate logical concepts such as "and," "or," "except when," "only when," and so on.

Material very heavy. Pace slow.

But it won't manipulate anything unless a man tells it how. Honeywell, whose aggressive EDP division has recently risen to become the nation's second-biggest computer maker, conducts a monthly programing seminar in a Boston suburb for top executives of its customer companies to help them understand what their EDP boys are gibbering about. The executives learn how to draw a "flow chart," agonizingly breaking down a problem-solving method into its smallest steps. They translate this flow chart into a set of instructions in a special, rigid, stilted English. (OPEN INPUT OMAST INVCRD. OPEN OUTPUT NMAST INVLST.) They watch a girl type out this semi-English version on a key-punch machine, which codes words and numbers in the form of holes punched into cards. These cards are fed into the computer, and another translation takes place. A canned "compiler" program (usually fed into the machine from a magnetic-tape unit) acts as an interpreter, translates the semi-English into logical statements in binary arithmetic. The computer finally does what the novice programmers have told it to do—if they've told it in the right way. The machine understands absolutely no deviations from its rigid language. Leave out so much as a comma, and it will either stop dead or go haywire. (At Cape Kennedy recently, a computer-guided rocket headed for Brazil instead of outer space because a programmer had left out a hyphen.) Finally, the executives head back to Boston's Logan International Airport, soothe their tired brains with ethyl alcohol with an olive or a twist, and morosely agree that nobody is so intractably, so maddeningly dense as a computer.

It's time to bring some people onstage. I'm still giving a lesson, but the people make it seem less like one.

Pace quickens.

This could all have been written without referring to Honeywell's executive seminar, but then it would have been too heavy to tolerate. The executives make it livelier.

And thus endeth the lesson —with a human scene.

But they are glad to have learned. They've

made a start toward finding out what goes on inside those strange square machines in the plant basement; and with that knowledge, they'll have a defense against a Machiavellian new kind of holdup that their Honeywell instructors have warned them about. It has happened more and more often and recently happened in one of the country's biggest publishing houses. Almost all the company's clerical work was computerized: inventory, billing, bookkeeping, payroll. With the corporate neurons thus inextricably tangled into the computer, the chief programmer went to the president and smilingly demanded that his salary be doubled. The president fired him on the spot—and shortly afterward realized the full enormity of what he had done. Nobody in the company, nobody in the whole world except the chief programmer knew what went on in the computer or how to make it do its work. The programs were too complex—and the computer, having no intelligence, could offer no explanations. As the horrified president now discovered, it was not true (as he had boasted) that a marvelous machine was running his company's paperwork. The cleverness hadn't been in the machine but in the brain of a man. With the man gone, the machine was just a pile of cold metal. The company nearly foundered in the ensuing year while struggling to unravel the mess.

Computers are that way: They absorb credit for human cleverness. Often a computerized operation will seem to go much more smoothly than it did in the old eyeshade-and-ledger days and the feeling will grow that the machine itself smoothed things out. What has really happened, however, is that the availability of the computer has forced human programmers to think logically about the operation and make it straightforward enough for the machine to handle. Professor David Johnson recalls a time when a company called him in to program an accounting operation for a computer. In previous years, this operation had taken two men ten months to perform by hand and brain. Johnson drew his flow charts, saw ways of simplifying, finally came up with an operation so organized that one man could do

V. HOW COMPUTERS ARE FALSELY PRAISED
Straight statement transition.

Blind anecdote with source identified.

Pace picks up more.

Statement transition uses key word "credit," which is what this whole section is about. The word will be echoed later.

Illustrative anecdote.

it in two days with a desk calculator. The company promptly abandoned its dreams of EDP— but if it had used a computer as planned, the machine rather than the programmer would doubtless have been showered with praise for the new simplicity.

Computers have been given credit for many things they haven't done. Even more, they've been given credit for things they were going to do in the future. The loudest crescendo of computer prognostications occurred in the late 1950s. Future-gazers went wild with enthusiasm. Soon, they said, computers would translate languages, write superb music, run libraries of information, become chess champions. Ah, those fantastic machines! Unfortunately, the whole history of computers—going all the way back to the pioneering Charles Babbage in the 19th Century—has been a series of manic-depressive cycles: early wild enthusiasm, followed by unexpected difficulties, followed by puzzled disappointment and silence.

Music? An amiable professor at the University of Illinois, Lejaren Hiller, Jr., has programed a machine to write music. One of the machine's compositions is the *Illiac Suite*. Says Hiller: "Critics have found it—er—interesting."

Chess? A computer in Russia is now engaged in a long-distance match with one at Stanford University in California. The match began awkwardly, with both machines making what for humans would be odd mistakes. Everybody concerned now seems somewhat embarrassed. Stanford's Professor of Computer Science John McCarthy, when asked recently how the game was going, said: "I have decided to put off any further interviews until the match is over."

Translate languages? There's something about human speech that computers just don't seem to get. It isn't rigid or formal enough; it's too subtle, too idiomatic. An IBM computer once translated "out of sight, out of mind" from English to Russian and back to English. The phrase returned to English as "blind, insane."

Libraries of information? "We don't know a good enough way to make a computer look up facts," says Honeywell programing researcher

---

Marginal notes:

Two-sentence transition uses a distant echo, "credit," twice. The transition gets me from past events to future predictions.

String-of-pearls interlude begins here. To effect transition from one pearl to the next, I use the recurring echo of a question mark.

Note my struggle to be specific in each case. All general statements are supported.

Sentences are short, pace fast. Article is starting downhill run toward end.

Roger Bender. He leans forward abruptly and jabs a finger at you. "Who wrote *Ivanhoe*?" he asks. You say, "Walter Scott." Bender says, "How did you know? Did you laboriously sort through books in your memory until you came to *Ivanhoe*? No. And how did you even know it was a book? You made the connections instantly, *and we don't know how.*"

Superbrains? Dr. Hubert L. Dreyfus, professor of philosophy at the Massachusetts Institute of Technology, recently published a paper called "Alchemy and Artificial Intelligence." In it, he expresses amusement at the prognosticators' claim that today's computers are "first steps" toward an ultimate smarter-than-human brain. The claim, he says, makes him think of a man climbing a tree, shouting, "Hey, look at me, I'm taking the first steps toward reaching the moon!" In fact, says Professor Dreyfus, computers don't and can't approximate human intelligence. They aren't even in the same league.

Even this near the end, I'm still introducing new authorities. The more an article contains, the more credible it is. Never ask the reader to believe your unsupported statements.

Honeywell's Roger Bender agrees. "We once had a situation where we wanted a machine to take a long list of numbers and find the highest number," he recalls. "Now, wouldn't that seem to you like an easy problem? Kids in first grade do it. Nobody has to tell them how. You just hand them a list and they look at the numbers and pick the highest. Of all the simple-minded —— well, it just shows what you have to go through with computers."

VI. ENDING
Quote transition gets me into last anecdote.

In this case, a programmer tried to figure out how he himself would tackle such a problem. He told the machine: "Start with the first number and go down the list until you come to a number that's higher. Store that number in memory. Continue until you find a still higher number," and so on. The last number stored would obviously (obviously to a man, that is) be the highest number on the list.

His quote was running long. To relieve monotony I stopped it here . . .

The machine imbibed its instructions, hummed for a while and stopped. It produced no answer.

"It was baffling," says Bender. "Nobody knew what the trouble was, until someone happened to glance down the list by eye. Then the problem became apparent. By great bad luck, it turned

. . . and resumed it here.

out, the highest number on the list was *the first number*. The computer simply couldn't figure out what to do about it."

Consultant John Diebold says: "Computers are enormously useful as long as you can predict in advance what the problems are going to be. But when something unexpected happens, the only computer in the world that's going to do you any good is the funny little one beneath your scalp."

Article stops dead, changes subjects and ends with a quote. Not really a summary, but a hard final statement that comes down with a nice thump.

C. Article for *TV Guide* Magazine

I've remarked several times in this book that an article writer must keep his eyes and ears wide open through every waking hour. You can't succeed in this profession unless you maintain a constant lookout for potential article ideas. This means talking to people, listening to them, seizing every chance to attend parties and dances and meetings and informal gatherings. It also means reading voraciously. Among other things, you should read at least one good newspaper every day, from the front page to the most trivial-looking news item buried in the back.

The article I am about to dissect for you grew from a little story half-buried among movie ads in the back pages of a newspaper. The story told about a judge in Sandusky, Ohio, who made use of television during the course of a trial. The judge's reasons weren't well explained; nor was the story long enough to say exactly how TV was applied to the courtroom procedure. But it was long enough to give me a glimpse of a potential magazine article.

You've got to know your markets. By reading every issue of every magazine you write for or hope to write for, you develop that subjective awareness of which ideas "feel" right for which magazines. This one felt right for *TV Guide*. In general, *TV Guide* concentrates on television as a broadcasting medium: it uses articles on famous TV personalities, on the popular shows, and so on. But occasionally it buys an article on television as a technological phenomenon. A would-be writer who had merely glanced at the magazine's covers or had casually flipped through a few issues would never have been aware of this. He would have thought, "Well, it's obviously a magazine about show biz. All the stories are about big names in New York and Hollywood." Only a writer who had read several months of issues thoroughly would have known what the magazine is really like.

It turned out, when I contacted *TV Guide,* that the editors had read about the Sandusky judge in their own Philadelphia newspapers and were also wondering about the article possibilities. (Yes, editors read newspapers too. Some read three newspapers a day, in fact.) They assigned the article to me.

There is another lesson for beginners here, I think. I live in Connecticut, far from Sandusky, Ohio. The editors gave me the assignment because I happened to be around at the right time and because they knew me (it was to be my eleventh *TV Guide* article). But I feel fairly certain that a writer living near Sandusky, even a beginner, would have had an excellent chance of selling the idea and getting a go-ahead—if he had acted before I did. Though in competition with established writers such as I, he would have had the advantage of proximity. Assuming he had learned his writing craft well and was able to submit a grade-A query, he might well have nailed down the assignment. He could have improved his chances by making a few phone calls before writing his query, and by including in it a few intriguing details that didn't appear in the brief newspaper accounts.

Good magazine article ideas crop up constantly in towns big and small, all over the country. Wherever you live, part of your self-assigned job as an article writer should be to watch closely the events in your vicinity—in fact, to get involved in those events as much as you can. Keep asking yourself, "Does this situation in my town have national significance? Can it be viewed as a microcosm or example of larger national events?"

If the answer is yes, use your proximity as a selling point when you write your query.

The research problems on this assignment were minor. This was not a survey article in any sense; there was no need to gather data from sources all over the country. The main source was obviously the Sandusky judge, whose name was James L. McCrystal. Other sources would be the lawyers, witnesses, jurors and others involved in the case—a relatively small group of people, all conveniently located in or near a single town.

I began the research by telephoning Judge McCrystal. As I had hoped, he was proud of what he had done and was delighted to hear from a journalist who proposed to tell the story in a major magazine. He invited me to come and see him. I think I could have interviewed him and everybody else by phone— and a beginning writer, lacking the freedom to travel, would almost certainly have tackled the job that way. But since I wanted to get away from my typewriter for a while, I went to Sandusky.

The judge and I spent an entire afternoon together. I came out of that interview with the feeling I knew everything I needed to know about the case. But an article writer should almost never be satisfied with a story drawn entirely from a single source. Such an article tends to have a "thin" sound. It reflects a certain laziness on the writer's part. The editors will think, "This writer hasn't done his homework. He hasn't cross-checked any facts or opinions. All he's told us is what one man says, and that one man may be exaggerating or distorting facts to make himself look good." *Playboy* and other magazines sometimes publish single-source, question-and-answer interviews, but that breed of article is rare. As a general rule, you should never allow yourself to be content with a single source. Thus, I talked to others beside the judge. When I wrote the article, I was careful to use their names.

I had a little trouble writing the lead. An anecdote lead is among the easiest kinds to handle, and I started by riffling through my notes in search of a good starting anecdote—one that would set the scene, hook the reader, do all the other jobs a good lead is supposed to do. I couldn't find an anecdote that was strong enough to take on the mission. I next hunted for a quote but failed again to find one that could do all the necessary jobs. I finally ended with a straightforward statement lead. We've noted before in this book that statement leads are often hard to pull off successfully and should generally be avoided unless you have something surprising to say. I felt then, and still feel today, that the lead I finally settled on was a little too flat. But it illustrates the truth that article writing, like life itself, is often a game of compromises.

Here is how the article appeared in the March 25, 1972, issue of *TV Guide*:

IS TELEVISION THE ANSWER FOR OUR CROWDED COURTS?

By MAX GUNTHER

Judge James L. McCrystal of Sandusky, Ohio, is a television fan. Under his auspices late last year, an entire trial was recorded on video tape and presented to the jury in the form of a TV show, neatly edited, condensed, telescoped down to its bare essentials. Such an experiment had never been tried before in this country or, as far as is known, anywhere in the world.

SECTION I: ESTABLISHMENT OF THEME
Lead language is somewhat cool, but subject matter is strong enough to grab the reader.

Many people, including the judge, were troubled by doubts about how well it would work and how the idea would be received in the legal community. Today those doubts are gone. That Sandusky trial is being discussed enthusiastically in courthouses all over this country and in Europe. And Judge McCrystal is discovering so many unexpected advantages in the TV-trial idea that it takes him the better part of an afternoon to enumerate them.

He is like a youngster on an Easter-egg hunt. Whenever he thinks he has finally turned up all

"Advantages" and "treasures" are what the article is about. A promise to the reader is implied here, and this promise will shape the article.

the treasures, somebody points to another one that he missed. He keeps hearing from other judges, lawyers, interested laymen. The writers and callers keep pointing to old and seemingly insoluble courtroom problems that might yield to a TV-trial approach. They keep saying, "You know, with that approach, we could . . ."

Judge McCrystal, a tall, calm man with a craggy face and cropped brown hair, has become busier and more famous than he really wants to be. But he is hugely pleased with the initial success of his idea. "We've started something here in Sandusky," he says contentedly. "We've demonstrated a whole new way to conduct a trial. There have been procedural changes in trials before, but this is the first *basic* change in the history of American law."

It all began as an obscure and perfectly ordinary traffic-accident case. Mrs. Mary Ann Clemens had lost control of her car and struck a pedestrian, Arthur McCall, injuring his shoulder and hand. McCall hired a young lawyer, Thomas Murray, Jr., to sue for damages on his behalf; and Mrs. Clemens hired an older lawyer, Raymond Watts, to defend her.

"We had the trial scheduled in the usual way," recalls young lawyer Murray, "but then a hitch developed. My client's medical witness, an osteopath, was going to be in Hawaii the week of the trial. I talked this over with the defendant's attorney and the judge, and we agreed that the thing to do was get the doctor's deposition on video tape before he left."

There was nothing unusual about this. Absent witnesses' statements can be written out and read in court, filmed or audio-recorded or, in recent years, recorded on TV tape. Courts in many states allow isolated parts of trials to be presented thus on TV.

But Judge McCrystal had a more far-reaching idea. Several months earlier, he had written an article for the Ohio Bar Journal in which he proposed conducting an entire trial through TV. "When I wrote it," he says, "I was mainly sug-

---

[Margin notes:]

A personal glimpse. The judge becomes more than a name.

SECTION II: SKETCHING IN THE BACKGROUND
The phrase "It all began . . ." signals a definite pause and transition.

A new source is introduced. I show I've done my homework.

In this section, notice the technique of switching back and forth from the writer's words to quoted words. This prevents monotony, adds credibility.

gesting a subject for discussion. But suddenly this little traffic case offered a perfect opportunity to try what I'd proposed."

He talked to the two lawyers, Murray and Watts. They agreed to go along with the experiment.

It happened that a man named Richard Reichert was working around the Erie County Courthouse at the time, installing some audio equipment. Reichert is vice president of an Ohio company called B&J Photo, Inc., which had had experience with video devices. The judge asked Reichert about the technical feasibility of the TV-trial idea. Reichert answered that, technically, what the judge wanted could be done.

Judge McCrystal then went to the Ohio Judicial Conference, a professional group composed of all judges in the state, and asked for money with which to conduct the experiment. This innovation-minded group was intrigued by his idea. "Very few professions have been as slow to change as the legal profession," says executive director Alan Whaling. "This isn't necessarily a criticism. In law it isn't wise to rush in new directions too fast. But it seemed to many that the time had come when this profession should be making greater use of modern technology." The group gave McCrystal $1000 to work with.

Videoman Reichert set up his camera and taping equipment in the courtroom, and the trial began without a jury. "We used no special lighting or anything else that might distract the witnesses," says Reichert. "Luckily, the natural light in that courtroom is pretty good. We were working with the simplest possible equipment, so we did have a few problems. We had no voltage regulators, for instance, and we'd get interference when the elevator in the building started up. But on the whole the picture quality turned out fine."

The plaintiff, defendant, witnesses, lawyers and judge all took their turns before the camera over a two-week period. There was no necessity for all to be present at the same time, as in a conventional trial, so each witness could show up at his

---

Always double-check name spellings. Only on the second check did I find "B&J" is spelled without periods.

Still another source appears . . .

. . . And another. The article is beginning to have the sound of solid research.

A minor generality—"we did have problems"—is supported by a specific example. Never let a generality hang alone.

own and the lawyers' convenience. Judge McCrystal didn't have to be present while the lawyers were questioning the witnesses.

When all the taping was done, the lawyers arranged the witnesses' testimony in proper order. Judge McCrystal then watched the "show" in his chambers. He studied the lawyers' objections to each other's questions. If he found a question improper, he had the question and the answer removed from the trial tape. (There was also a master tape which was left untouched.) If he decided to overrule an objection, he had the objection itself removed. Thus the final tape contained none of the usual courtroom histrionics in which a lawyer says something he knows is improper, and the judge tells the jurors to disregard it, and everybody knows they can't and won't.

The trial was now ready for the jury. On a prearranged day the 12 citizens arrived at the courthouse. They listened to live opening statements from the lawyers, then watched the two-and-a-half-hour show on two 18-inch TV screens. The judge and lawyers were free to attend to other business throughout that time. The jurors reached their verdict on that same day (McCall was awarded $9600) and were home in time for supper.

Everybody involved—including the losing lawyer—considered the experiment a nearly perfect success. So did many outside observers. Each had his own reasons to be pleased.

Judge McCrystal and other judges were particularly happy with the time saved. "Court calendars everywhere are badly clogged," says C. William O'Neill, Chief Justice of the Ohio Supreme Court. "The televison approach could allow a much more efficient use of judges' time."

Indeed it could. Enormous amounts of time are wasted in conventional court procedures, for the judge must be physically present throughout each trial. A judge might arrive at his courthouse at 9 A.M. and find that, of the four trials he had scheduled that day, two have been settled out of

> Using quote marks like this is sometimes necessary, but once per article is plenty. It has an amateurish look if overdone.

> SECTION III: ENUMERATING THE ADVANTAGES
> I now settle down to fulfill the promise made in Section I. The article from here on will be essentially a list of the "treasures." Its structure is determined by the promise.

> Advantage #1.

court and the other two need to be continued because doctors can't make it to testify. Thus,
despite his huge case load, the judge must waste
another day. But if all trials were video-taped,
he could work on them as his time became available. He need not be present while each pair of
lawyers questioned witnesses in each case. Finding one trial postponed, he would simply pick up
the next set of tapes.

The jurors were equally pleased with their
own saving of time. They would have had to come
back for at least a second day if the case had been
conducted in the conventional way. "Usually
we're happy if we can occupy 60 per cent of a
jury's time," says James Young, executive director of the Ohio Legal Institute. "They spend
the other 40 per cent just sitting around waiting.
The judge confers with the lawyers, or he's called
to the phone, or one of the lawyers can't find a
document. But with TV, you show the jury only
what's essential."

The two lawyers in the case were delighted
with the time-saving factor from their own point
of view. "Obviously I wasn't wildly happy with
the end result," says Raymond Watts, the defendant's attorney. "But it was a fair trial. And
the idea offers a new kind of flexibility because
you don't have to gather a big group of people in
the same place at the same time. I have a trial
scheduled in New York this coming fall, for
instance. It happens that's an inconvenient time
for me. It would be great if I could go to New
York and tape the material at my own and the
other people's convenience."

Lawyers, like judges, could handle more cases
if they could schedule their time more flexibly
in this way. It's conceivable that they could then
reduce the fees charged to each client. It is
nearly certain that doctors and other so-called
"expert witnesses" could cut their court-appear-
ance fees for televised trials. At present, lawyers
prefer doctors to appear in the flesh whenever
possible on the theory that a televised or audio-
recorded witness loses impact in an otherwise

Advantage #2.

Another new source appears.

Advantage #3.
*Note the transition tech-
nique. It would have been
monotonous if I had kept
on saying, "Another advantage is . . ."*

#4.

live trial. A doctor who must spend the better part of a day getting to a courthouse and back may charge several hundred dollars for his time. But if an entire trial were televised, there would be no need to ask the doctor to appear in person and he could charge less.

Judge McCrystal believes the TV-trial approach will not only increase the speed of justice and cut the cost, but will improve the quality at the same time. "We can cut out all the courtroom byplay," he says, "all the improper questions, the 'disregard this' and 'disregard that.' We can present the jury with the distilled facts of a case, not the maneuverings and personalities of the lawyers." #5.

Lawyers Murray and Watts both agree. Says Watts: "Suppose you're up against the kind of lawyer who likes to throw curve balls. You've got to keep jumping up and objecting. After a while the jury begins to get mad at you. With TV, neither the other guy's improper tactics nor your objections would show up on the final tape."

The witnesses themselves felt they stated their cases better before the quiet, unjudging eye of a TV camera than they might before a live jury. Arthur McCall, a shy and soft-spoken man, remarked at one point that he would have been nervous with 12 jurors and a courtroom audience staring at him. He and his lawyer both felt he came across well as a "two-dimensional plaintiff" (the term now being used throughout Ohio), while he might have frozen and become ineffectual in a live courtroom situation. "He speaks very softly," says lawyer Murray. "He might not have been heard at all in a conventional trial. On TV he appeared very much the way he is in everyday life, natural, relaxed." #6.

As for videoman Reichert, he too came away happy. The bill he rendered for his services was $362. This included rental of Sony equipment, the cost of half-inch tapes, and travel and hotel expenses for equipment operators—about a third of the money Judge McCrystal had available for the experiment. "We showed that televised trials needn't be expensive," says Reichert. #7. Note that I'm still avoiding the monotony of using the word "advantage" over and over again.

He thinks some improvements are possible the next time around. "One thing I'd like to do," he says, "is tape witnesses at their homes or elsewhere instead of doing them all in the same courtroom. This way we'll get some changes of scene, make it more interesting for the jury."

Some incidental material appears here. This paragraph could have been cut if the editors had been cramped for space.

Reichert seems quite sure there will be a next time. He is now in the process of setting up a new company specifically for courtroom TV. Several such companies already do exist in Ohio and other states. So far their work has been confined mainly to taping depositions of isolated witnesses who can't make it to court. Reichert believes his company will earn at least some of its income by televising entire trials.

So could this one.

His optimism seems well founded. Judge McCrystal is already planning a second TV trial—this one involving an accident at a railroad switch. The plan is to send a camera crew out to the scene and let the jury see it instead of merely hearing about it.

And this one.

The judge ponders still more advantages that may be gained in future trials. "TV will help us solve some of the problems of long delays," he says. "We had a case here recently where I would have loved to use the TV approach. The case involved an injury to a child's eye. The doctor said it would take several years before he could tell how serious the injury was, so I had to grant a long continuance. When that case finally gets back to court years from now, who knows where all the witnesses will be? Some may be dead. Others may not remember the events clearly anymore. Wouldn't it be a good idea to get them all on tape right now and store the tapes until they're needed?"

After a short breather, we're back to the list of advantages. This is #8.

A specific case story brightens the prose. I felt the long list of advantages might be growing monotonous.

A few groups have been cool to the TV-trial idea. One is the American Bar Association, which so far has refrained from commenting officially. "We feel more time will be needed to study this whole question," says a spokesman. In general, ABA has long been opposed to any kind of photography or video in courtrooms. Its canon of ethics says cameras "detract from the essential dignity of the proceedings" and may "distract participants."

I've now listed eight advantages. My promise is fulfilled.

SECTION IV: WINDING DOWN
It is important to keep the article from being a mere eulogy. Hence, some negative material for balance.

Court stenographers are also worried, for they fear their jobs may disappear if trials are recorded on TV instead of by written transcript. Judge McCrystal thinks their fears are unfounded. "This video equipment is so simple that anyone can learn to operate it in short order," he says. "A court stenographer could become a court videoman. He would simply change equipment, not lose his function."

More negative reactions.

The judge doesn't feel TV trials will be used in criminal cases for many years, if ever. "The whole field of criminal law is so full of doubts and uncertainties right now," says the judge, "that to introduce the TV idea into it would only be to stir up a new hornet's nest of questions. I feel we should move slowly in that area."

Everyone else in and around Sandusky seems to agree. "But civil trials are what mainly clog the courts," says lawyer Murray. "As a ball-park guess, I'd say at least 50 per cent of all court time is taken up by auto-accident cases. If we can speed up just those cases, that alone will oil the whole system."

An upbeat.

Even if there were no legal objections to the use of TV in criminal cases, there might be some pretty loud grousing from nonlegal sources. The popular lawyer shows we now watch on our home tubes could be abruptly stripped of half their dramatic possibilities. When you settled down for an evening's entertainment, you might find yourself watching TV shows about people watching TV shows.

I'm still trying to balance what has been a generally "gee-whiz" article. To preserve my journalistic detachment, I close with a grin.